Praise for *Intrinsi*

After many decades of working on the climate crisis, I'm someone who hope does not come naturally to every day. these pages all the more valuable to me, and

— Bill McKibben
co-founder

There is no healing or transformation withou of global crisis that breed denial, hopelessness and despair. This deeply wise book guides us in nurturing the "intrinsic hope" that evolves our consciousness and frees our heart to act on behalf of this world we love.

— Tara Brach, author of *Radical Acceptance* and *True Refuge*

If you feel despair for our endangered world, read this remarkable book and then act. Saving ourselves and much of life on Earth requires us to take brave and visionary action, but doing *that* requires hope—the kind that arises from the depths of our own human psyches, from our souls, and from Earth herself. Assisting us to tap this crucial resource is what Kate Davies accomplishes with her love-offering of *Intrinsic Hope*. This wise, adeptly crafted, inspiring, and practical book deepens and amplifies our capacities as agents of cultural renaissance and executors of ecological regeneration.

—Bill Plotkin, Ph.D., author of *Soulcraft* and *Wild Mind*

Kate Davies' book *Intrinsic Hope: Living Courageously in Troubled Times* is a fresh and inspirational guide for practicing deep ecology. Her ideas about hope and the tools she offers to nurture it ground us in the Earth's inherent goodness and provide a path forward when everything seems to be falling apart. That inherent goodness—intrinsic hope—lives within each one of us, as well as in all life. In this book, Kate shows us how to access it and how to take action based on it. I cannot recommend *Intrinsic Hope* highly enough.

— John Seed, founder and director of the
Rainforest Information Centre and
co-author of *Thinking Like a Mountain:
Towards a Council of All Beings.*

We are becoming aware that the eco-social crisis is not only an external reality, but also an internal psychological, spiritual and moral crisis. In order to survive the increasing devastation, hope is essential. Kate Davies explores the psychological and spiritual dimensions of "intrinsic hope" and how it can be a light to guide us in these darkening times. Her book contains valuable insights into our inner landscapes and describes the qualities we need if we are to survive and live together on this Earth, full of wonder, beauty and love.

— Llewellyn Vaughan-Lee, Ph.D., Sufi teacher
and author of *Spiritual Ecology: The Cry of the Earth*.

Kate Davies' whole working life and career has led to this distillation of "intrinsic hope." Her experience as scientist, as Quaker, as mother and activist forged a commitment to reject despair and forge a new, more resilient type of hope. This is a prescription in a book we all need.

— Elizabeth May, OC, Leader of the Green Party of Canada
and Member of Parliament for Saanich-Gulf Islands.

To be an activist you have to be an optimist. *Intrinsic Hope: Living Courageously in Troubled Times* confirms this conviction. In her inspiring book, Kate Davies explores the state of our planet and the way we can transform our present predicament into positive possibilities. This beautifully written book weaves together the practical with the political, the social with the spiritual and economical with the ecological. It is a remarkable achievement!

— Satish Kumar, Editor Emeritus, *Resurgence & Ecologist* Magazine.

Have you ever read a book that is so wise and so important that you immediately recommend it to your friends? Have you ever read a book so full of transformative insights and brilliant aphorisms that you underline and dog-ear and exclaim YES in ink all over the margins? *Intrinsic Hope: Living Courageously in Troubled Times* is such a book. In a time of terrible peril, and so a time of deep and debilitating despair, Kate Davies powerfully, convincingly re-invents hope, just when we need it the most.

— Kathleen Dean Moore, author of *Great Tide Rising*
and *Piano Tide*, winner of the 2017
Willa Cather Award for contemporary fiction

Being mindful of hope may be our most urgent challenge in the face of growing eco-social problems. Kate Davies points toward multiple ways to activate hope. May her book be read by many who are seeking a path forward into the arena of transformative change.

— Mary Evelyn Tucker, Yale Forum on Religion and Ecology

intrinsic hope

living courageously
in troubled times

by Kate Davies, M.A., D. Phil.

new society
PUBLISHERS

Cover design by Diane McIntosh.
Cover image: © iStock 532520587.
Text: p. xiii © YB, p. 17 © Dmitry/Adobe Stock.

Printed in Canada. First printing April, 2018

Inquiries regarding requests to reprint all or part of *Intrinsic Hope*
should be addressed to New Society Publishers at the address below.
To order directly from the publishers, please call toll-free (North America)
1-800-567-6772, or order online at www.newsociety.com

Any other inquiries can be directed by mail to:

New Society Publishers
P.O. Box 189, Gabriola Island, BC V0R 1X0, Canada
(250) 247-9737

LIBRARY AND ARCHIVES CANADA CATALOGUING IN PUBLICATION

Davies, Kate, 1956–, author

Intrinsic hope : living courageously in troubled times / by Kate Davies,
M.A., D. Phil.

Includes bibliographical references and index.
Issued in print and electronic formats.
ISBN 978-0-86571-867-8 (softcover).—ISBN 978-1-55092-660-6 (PDF).—
ISBN 978-1-77142-255-0 (EPUB)

1. Hope. 2. Human ecology—Psychological aspects. 3. Environmental
degradation—Psychological aspects. I. Title.

BD216.D38 2018   128   C2017-907042-8
                                                   C2017-907043-6

Funded by the Government of Canada | Financé par le gouvernement du Canada

New Society Publishers' mission is to publish books that contribute in fundamental
ways to building an ecologically sustainable and just society, and to do so with the least
possible impact on the environment, in a manner that models this vision.

new society PUBLISHERS

Certified B Corporation

FSC MIX Paper from responsible sources FSC® C016245

Contents

Part II: Habits of Hope

Foreword

Hope—like faith, love, and charity—is just a word until the truth of it actually enters our lives, often through a crisis. My own understanding was superficial until, in 2004, I was diagnosed with Stage 3 colon cancer.

Strangely, I felt more relieved than frightened. Hearing the sentence no one ever wants to hear, I surprised myself with a sense of humor—and sass. I didn't battle cancer. I didn't try to get back to anything. I wasn't even trying to survive. Rather, I entered it and dove under the surface of what to all appearances was a successful and meaningful life. I wanted to find my true self, whether I lost my life or not.

With officially less than 50% chance of survival and on the advice of two naturopaths, I began a 6-round protocol of chemotherapy. Because of a dream that said "…, by water I will be healed," I'd moved into a basic one-room house teetering on a cliff overlooking Puget Sound and Mt. Rainier. I needed the twice daily 20-foot tides to wash my soul.

If you've had chemo or supported someone going through it, you know it is an indignity. My body rejected it in ways the docs had not before seen. One day as I lay on the floor near the bathroom awaiting the every quarter hour expulsion of the poison, I noticed the absence of something I'd had my whole life and never knew it. What left me was like a seventh sense: a sense of the future. I wasn't afraid of dying, of having no future in the future. Rather, I saw in that moment that the future is actually a need of the soul like water is a need of the body. In disappearing, the future revealed itself as a necessary fiction, not a reality. In the absence of this sense of the future, thought stopped. It was not Nirvana. It was stark, yet reassuringly real. I saw that anything we build in our lives—love, learning, work, relationships, and so forth—we must generate sense of the future. Hope is a creative act, a product of soul, will, and imagination. It is projection from within us, not a movie we are watching with baited breath.

For a dreamer, writer, social innovator like me, the collapse of the space into which to create was like a death. It was like hitting bottom. From that moment forward, I knew that any hope I might feel about anything was actually my creation, not my future prospects. And so, in the months ahead, I rebuilt the space into which my life would continue to unfold.

Hope in Spanish is the same word as wait. Espero que te vaya bien. I hope all goes well for you. Te espero en la esquina. I'll wait for you at the corner. In an old hymn they say, "those that wait upon the Lord will be renewed in strength." Hope then is more of an expectancy than an expectation. A willingness to be empty, to not know and yet to not fear.

Fast forward a few years. At a meditation retreat, I couldn't shake a world weariness that blanketed my mood like a weight on my shoulders and lungs. An image hung in my mind of an exhausted warrior after too many battles, praying to be released from this body. She who had been fueled by a conviction that we can win on important issues could only see a dreary futility ahead based on a dreary assessment of the past. Embracing rather than resisting this experience, I seemed to wake up with a start. Who is this stranger inhabiting me? Not only was I indulging myself, like Job in the Bible I'd projected my weariness on the world. The last thing anyone needed, especially the young people now turning towards me, was my despair. Nearing my seventh decade, my role was not to litter their minds with stories of my own failures, but rather to hold open that sense of the future I'd created for myself years earlier. I needed to *be* hope for the generations behind me as they engaged in the tough, confusing work of finding their way.

Not to be hopeful *for* them, but to have an abiding faith their capacity to build a future beyond what I could imagine.

Then another truth showed up. What do I actually know about "the future" anyway? In truth I don't know what's going to happen even an hour from now! Hopelessness *about*, like hope *for*, is a fiction, and one that needs to be pulped.

These and other experiences shifted my relationship with hope from a struggle to change "the world" I imagined and took for reality, transforming even my sense of there being someone or something to place my hopes in. Instead, I found beauty in an open and empowered trust in myself and others—especially our youth—to meet what life presents.

In this magnificent and timely book Kate Davies systematically turns our attention from "hoping for" to hope as an intrinsic quality of our inner being that radiates from us. It is our gift. She transmutes hope for the future into trust in ourselves an relationship with whatever comes. We become sturdy and peaceful rather than anxious and stuck. The practices she suggests turn our attention to this presence, out of which we again rise and rise to occasions large and small. We need intrinsic hope in these challenging and unpredictable times. Cutting through the din of crushing analyses and the triviality of panaceas, Kate offers a lucid and empowering framework.

— Vicki Robin
October 2017
Whidbey Island

[Hope] is the presentiment that imagination is more real and reality is less real than it looks. It is the hunch that the overwhelming brutality of facts that oppress and repress us is not the last word. It is the suspicion that reality is more complex than the realists want us to believe. That the frontiers of the possible are not determined by the limits of the actual; and in a miraculous and unexplained way life is opening up creative events which will open the way to freedom and resurrection—but the two—suffering and hope must live from each other. Suffering without hope produces resentment and despair. But, hope without suffering creates illusions, naïveté and drunkenness.

So let us plant dates even though we who plant them will never eat them. We must live by the love of what we will never see. That is the secret discipline. It is the refusal to let our creative act be dissolved away by our need for immediate sense experience and is a struggled commitment to the future of our grandchildren. Such disciplined hope is what has given prophets, revolutionaries and saints, the courage to die for the future they envisage. They make their own bodies the seed of their highest hopes.

— Rubem Alves, *Tomorrow's Child: Imagination, Creativity, and the Rebirth of Culture*

Introduction:
Where On Earth
Are We Going?

IN EARLY 2015, I was on Haleakala on the Hawaiian island of Maui. At just over ten thousand feet, it is Maui's tallest volcano. From the summit, the landscape below looked harsh and inhospitable. Bleak black lava fields stretched into the distance and there was an almost complete lack of vegetation. A biting wind sliced through the layers of warm clothing I had put on earlier that morning. In this desolate place, my attention was drawn to an endangered nēnē goose walking slowly across the trail about 50 yards in front of me. A fellow visitor also noticed the inconspicuous grey-brown bird and we struck up a conversation. After talking about the nēnē and our surroundings, he told me he was a recently retired steel worker from the east coast and this trip to Hawaii had been on his bucket list for years. Then he asked me what I did. After I told him that I taught environmental studies and sustainability, he sighed deeply and looked away as his eyes filled with tears. In a soft and sorrowful voice, he proceeded to tell me about his only son and daughter-in-law who had lost their home to Hurricane Sandy in 2012. The storm surge had destroyed their New Jersey shoreline house and although it had been rebuilt, the young couple had not fully recovered. They had become so alarmed about climate disruption they decided not to have any children, so he will never have grandchildren. This broke his heart.

A few months later, I was teaching a class at Antioch University Seattle. The students and I were talking about recent environmental changes they had noticed. A twenty-something-year-old talked about going to Alaska every summer and noticing how much the glaciers were receding from year to year. Another spoke about the decline in salmon and steelhead populations and what it meant for his tribe. Then someone else told about her Australian friends who had decided to immigrate to the Pacific Northwest because of the now unbearable summer heat in their home country. Gradually, the conversation lapsed into silence. Then a young woman quietly said, "It's all too much. I am terrified about what's happening and I don't know where it's all going. I don't have much hope for the future." Her words tailed off as she began to cry, tears coursing down her pretty face. Some of her colleagues looked away and shuffled their papers, embarrassed by her show of emotion. Others nodded their heads in agreement because she had given voice to their unspoken thoughts.

Retired steel workers, students, and many others are beginning to express their feelings about the state of the environment. They know something is terribly wrong. Their experience is consistent with the scientific consensus that humankind is destroying the earth's ecosystems and threatening the future of life on the planet. Although scientists have been saying this for decades, what's happening now is different because ordinary people are witnessing the changes for themselves. Whether they are losing their homes to hurricanes, floods, wildfires, or rising sea levels, enduring extreme heat or cold, living with drought or getting sick from pollution, what's happening now could be a game-changer. Even many who are only affected indirectly are becoming alarmed.

Indeed, concern about climate disruption has already led hundreds of thousands of people to protest. In September 2014, about 600,000 people in more than 160 countries around the world took to the streets, including about 400,000 in New York City alone. A similar number voiced their concern just over a year later just ahead of the 2015 Paris Agreement on climate change. And in April 2017, over 200,000 people turned out in Washington, D.C., and tens of thousands more took part at over 370 sister marches worldwide. Even though the truth is very inconvenient, it's beginning to change the way people think, feel, and act.

The Global Eco-social Crisis and Its Impacts

It's only in the past few decades that humankind has woken up to the fact that there is an emerging global eco-social crisis. Before then, people thought about environmental problems as if they were separate from each other and contained within specific geographical boundaries. But now local issues tend to be seen in a larger context—a drought can remind us about climate disruption, the destruction of a wetland can remind us about worldwide habitat loss, dead fish in a lake can remind us about pollution's global scale. There's also a growing realization that action on any one issue won't be effective unless it is connected to actions on others. For example, you can't work on preserving biodiversity without working on habitat destruction, climate disruption, invasive species, pollution, human overpopulation, and overharvesting, and you can't work to prevent habitat destruction without working on food production, agricultural practices, lumber harvesting, housing and infrastructure development, water availability, and pollution. Perhaps most significantly, there's an increasing recognition that environmental problems cannot be treated separately from their social, cultural, and economic contexts. For instance, communities of color are often exposed to higher levels of toxic chemicals, and climate disruption affects vulnerable populations more than others. As John Muir, founder of the Sierra Club, said "When we try to pick out anything by itself, we find it hitched to everything else in the Universe."[1]

Because the scale of the crisis is still sinking in, there is not yet an agreed word or phrase to describe it. In this book, I use the expression "global eco-social crisis" because it underscores the systemic and interconnected nature of our problems, as well as their urgency. When I use it, I include all environmental problems and their social, cultural, and economic contexts. I believe that focusing exclusively on any single problem, even climate disruption, oversimplifies our predicament. In addition, I have chosen to use the phrase "climate disruption" rather than the more neutral "climate change" or the seemingly benign "global warming." This is because, to me, climate disruption better describes the nature of the changes that we are beginning to witness.

"Global eco-social crisis" may be appropriate but it feels overwhelming. Speaking personally, I find it impossible to fully grasp its magnitude, even though I have spent the past 35 years of my life working on eco-social problems. For starters, there's climate disruption, resource depletion, pollution, species extinction, habitat loss, water scarcity, and population growth. Then there's all their local, regional, and global manifestations. And then there's all the ways these problems intersect with other issues, such as poverty, unemployment, racism, and health. Put everything together and it's completely mind-boggling. Even if I were to try to catalogue all the evidence of harm, I suspect you would feel as overwhelmed as I do. So instead, here are just a few facts and figures to illustrate where we are and where we may be going:

+ **Climate disruption.** Considered the largest single threat to human survival, climate disruption is already causing severe heat waves, droughts, floods, hurricanes, tornadoes, and wildfires throughout the world, as well as rising sea levels, ocean acidification, desertification, erosion, reduced food production, shifts in species ranges, and effects on human health.[2] By the end of this century, global temperatures are expected to rise by between 0.3 to 4.8 degrees Celsius,[3] significantly exacerbating these effects and changing life on earth as we know it.

+ **Water scarcity.** About 700 million people living in 43 countries suffer from water scarcity. By 2015, 1.8 billion people will be living in countries or regions with absolute water scarcity, and two thirds of the world's population could be living under water stressed conditions. With the existing climate change scenario, almost half the world's population will be living in high water stress by 2030.[4] Water scarcity is already regarded as a major threat to world security by the US intelligence community.[5]

+ **Species extinction.** Nearly one quarter of all mammalian species and about one in eight bird species are likely to become extinct in the next 30 years. In the past 40 years, populations of vertebrate animals—such as mammals, birds, and fish—have declined by a whopping 58 percent.[6] The current rate of biodiversity loss is between 1,000 and 10,000 times greater than the natural rate.[7]

+ **Pollution.** Pollution is now ubiquitous. There is nowhere on the planet that is uncontaminated. Some of the highest levels are in the Arctic, many thousands of miles away from any direct sources. The world's cities already generate about 1.3 billion metric tonnes of solid waste per year and this is expected to increase to 2.2 billion metric tonnes by 2025.[8] Wastes pollute the air, land, and water. Between 4.8 and 12.7 million metric tonnes of plastic ends up in the oceans, where it harms wildlife and damages marine ecosystems.[9] By 2050, the weight of plastic in the world's oceans will exceed the weight of fish.[10]

+ **Environmental injustice.** Environmental injustice is widespread and getting worse. Developed countries exploit developing countries by grabbing their natural resources, building hazardous facilities and using them as a dumping ground for toxic waste, and coercing them into wildlife conservation measures without regard for the people who live in or close to protected areas. Within countries, including the US, racial minorities and people living in poverty are often exposed to higher levels of pollution and greater risks.[11]

+ **Population growth and consumerism.** The world's population is already 7.6 billion and it is expected to increase to 11.1 billion by 2100.[12] At the same time, billions in the developing world are adopting the consumer lifestyle of developed countries. These two trends are putting increasing stress on the planet's already depleted natural resources.

These facts and figures may seem remote and abstract from your daily life, but they represent very real problems with very real implications for your health and wellbeing.

We all rely on the earth's life support systems for every breath we take, every sip of water we drink, and every mouthful of food we eat. Quite simply, human existence depends on the earth. No ifs, ands, or buts. When we damage the environment, we damage ourselves. In the words widely attributed to Chief Seattle, "The earth does not belong to man, man belongs to the earth. All things are connected like the blood that unites us all. Man did not weave the web of life, he is merely a strand in it. Whatever man does to the web, he does to himself."[13] To put it succinctly, human health depends on a healthy planet or as ecotheologian Thomas Berry said, "You cannot have well humans on a sick planet."[14]

There is very strong scientific evidence that human health and wellbeing are already affected by environmental quality. According to the World Health Organization, nearly one quarter of all human disease is due to poor environmental quality[15]—almost half of all asthma, about one fifth of all cancers, about one sixth of all cardiovascular disease, and one twentieth of all birth defects. The proportion is even higher for children. This burden of disease causes indescribable human pain and suffering, as well as an untold loss of human happiness and productivity. Tragically, most of it could be prevented.

But that's not all. The damage we inflict on the environment comes back to harm us in other ways. In 1992, I was living in Canada when overfishing destroyed the North Atlantic cod fishery. The industry that had sustained the island of Newfoundland and many small mainland communities for more than 500 years suddenly vanished when the fishery crashed to about one percent of its former size. The socio-economic consequences were enormous. In the immediate aftermath, more than 35,000 fishermen and plant workers from over 400 coastal communities lost their jobs[16] and a $500 million a year industry[17] disappeared virtually overnight. Many people lost the only source of income they had ever known and became dependent on hastily assembled government welfare programs. The demise of the North Atlantic cod fishery destroyed a way of life and led to a massive emigration of young people and families that devastated many towns and villages. Only now, some 25 years later, are the fish beginning to return. This example and others, including the US Dust Bowl of the 1930s, the destruction of the Amazon rainforest, and the virtual disappearance of the Aral Sea in central Asia, reveal that "environmental" disasters are never just environmental disasters. They always affect people and communities, and often entire societies.

It's true that a few societies have survived horrendous environmentally-related catastrophes. In the mid-1300s, rats carrying the Plague spread rapidly across Europe, leading to the death of somewhere between 30 and 50 percent of the human population—between 25 and 40 million people.[18,19] But despite this enormous loss of life and its terrible socio-economic consequences, the Renaissance flourished. But sadly, compete social collapse is a more common consequence. Examples in this category include the people of Easter Island and the Mayan culture, who overexploited their natural resources, and the Norse of Greenland, who destroyed fragile Northern ecosystems and failed to adapt to an increasingly harsh climate.[20] In these cases, entire societies perished because of an unwillingness to accept evidence of environmental deterioration and take appropriate action.

But what's happening now is not about a single society or culture. We are witnessing the onset of a global eco-social crisis that threatens the future of our species and many others. Moreover, we know this one is human-caused. Unlike earlier catastrophes, this one cannot be blamed on ignorance, vengeful gods, or other supernatural forces. We know we are responsible. These three factors— its global scale, its threat to the future of life on earth, and the knowledge that we caused it—mark this crisis as unprecedented in human history.

Psychological Impacts

Although there is a lot of scientific information about the unfolding crisis and how it will affect human health and wellbeing, we know very little about its psychological impacts. So far, few in-depth studies have been done on this important topic. One source of information is public opinion polling. Even though it is a superficial and unreliable surrogate it does indicate significant levels of concern, and that people around the world are worried. In China, about 80 percent of the population is concerned about the country's environmental problems.[21] In Brazil, 87 percent believe that climate change is "very serious."[22] In Australia, a survey of children reported that over half were worried about not having enough water, almost half said they were anxious about climate change, and a similar proportion said they were concerned about air and water pollution.[23]

But the psychological impacts of the global eco-social crisis go far beyond concern, worry, and anxiety and include much more serious disorders. Three main types can be identified:

- Direct and acute effects associated with living through extreme weather events and other environmental disasters. These include acute and post traumatic stress disorder, depression, despair, grief, place attachment disorder, apathy, fear, somatic disorders, drug and alcohol use, and suicide.

- Indirect or vicarious effects associated with observing these events combined with uncertainty about the future. These include fear, guilt, sadness, despair, depression, anger, grief, and apathy.
- Community or large-scale psychosocial effects. These include decreased community cohesion, a disrupted sense of continuity and belonging, increased violence and crime, increased social instability, increased interpersonal and intergroup aggression, and domestic abuse.

As conditions deteriorate, these impacts are likely to become more common. In the US, one recent study predicted that two hundred million Americans will experience serious psychological impacts from climate disruption and that in many instances the distress will be severe.[24] Even the conservative American Psychological Association, the world's largest professional association of psychologists, is warning about the mental health consequences of climate disruption.[25]

These psychological effects are to be expected. Like other animals, human beings get extremely frightened whenever our survival is threatened. However, this crisis isn't just about our individual survival, it's about our collective survival. Ecopsychologist Joanna Macy calls this realization "the pivotal psychological reality of our time." She says, "Every generation throughout history lived with the tacit certainty that there would be generations to follow. Each assumed, without questioning, that its children and children's children would walk the same earth, under the same sky. Hardships, failures, and personal death were encompassed in that vaster assurance of continuity. That certainty is now lost to us, whatever our politics. That loss, unmeasured and immeasurable, is the pivotal psychological reality of our time."[26]

This terrifying reality is more difficult to accept because we don't talk about it. When we fail to acknowledge our feelings about the future, they don't go away. Exactly the opposite happens—they fester in our unconscious and get worse. And the more we avoid talking about our feelings, the more isolated and alone we feel, and the more we can think that our feelings are abnormal or unfounded. But these emotions are very natural. Indeed, from an evolutionary perspective, they have been hardwired into us as a survival mechanism, constituting an internal early warning system. We ignore them at our peril. Vietnamese Buddhist monk Thich Nhat Hanh calls them "the bells of mindfulness." He says "[t]he bells of mindfulness are calling out to us, trying to wake us up, reminding us to look deeply at our impact on the planet."[27] However unpleasant or unwanted, these feelings are telling us that we urgently need to change our ways. Indeed, unless we heed them and wake up, we may not survive.

We can hear Thich Nhat Hanh's bells of mindfulness and feel the earth's suffering because we are part of her. It's as if we are the cells of her body and can feel the trauma she is experiencing. No one is isolated or separate from her so it is only natural that everyone is affected by what's happening to the environment—whether we acknowledge it or not. If we see an oil-covered pelican struggling for its life, the raw stumps of a clear-cut forest, or a smokestack belching pollution into the atmosphere, we feel sad. We experience these feelings because we are connected to the earth—not just physically but at the deepest levels of our humanity.

The Psychological Context

It would be easier if we could separate our feelings about the global eco-social crisis from our feelings about everything else that's happening. But life isn't like that. The pain we feel about the destruction of the environment is amplified by the pain we feel about other things. Speaking personally, my sadness about the global eco-social crisis is exacerbated by sadness about all the wars, aggression, bigotry, and injustice in the world. As well as the damage we are inflicting on the earth, there has never been so much violence and the number of armed conflicts between and within countries continues to increase.[28] Many national economies are in crisis, social welfare programs are being cut, corruption is increasing, and the disparity between rich and poor keeps getting larger. A new wave of racism, intolerance, isolationism, and competitive individualism is sweeping across North America and Europe, to say nothing about what's happening in the Middle East, parts of Africa, and Russia. Given all of this, it's easy for me to feel hopeless.

Meanwhile, at an individual level many people feel their lives are becoming more stressful. Anxiety and depression are reaching epidemic proportions in many countries. In the US, forty million people suffer from anxiety[29] and almost 13 percent are on antidepressants.[30] In the UK, it's a similar story, with about one in five adults affected by anxiety or depression.[31] It seems as if life is spinning out of control. There's less and less time and more and more to do. People feel overscheduled, overcommitted, and overextended. Ask someone how they are and they will likely answer "super busy," "crazy busy," or "insanely busy." There's no time to relax, talk with friends and neighbors, go for a walk, read a book, or simply do nothing at all. From dawn to dusk and beyond, many of us rush from task to task and as soon as there's any pause in the action we are busy checking email, texting, or tweeting. I don't have to go into detail about all the sources of stress and anxiety in everyday life. Chances are, you experience them for yourself.

So with all of this as background, where on earth are we going?

Where On Earth Are We Going?

Given the growing severity of the global eco-social crisis and its impacts, one place we seem to be heading is towards becoming a hopelessness society. Ordinary people are feeling increasingly pessimistic about the future of life on earth, humankind's future, and their own personal futures. Expectations that tomorrow will be better than today no longer seem realistic and the hope that everything will turn out OK seems increasingly naïve.

Many people still hope that new technology will save us. It's easy to see why. Over the past 200 years, technology has improved the quality and quantity of human life enormously. Immunization has saved countless children from early death. Pasteurization, refrigeration, and other food processing techniques have made the food supply much safer and more reliable. Drinking water chlorination and sewage treatment have dramatically reduced the rates of many waterborne diseases. In the past 20 years, there have been amazing advances in renewable energy, green building, seawater desalination, phyto- and microbial remediation, and green chemistry.

Even though these and other recent innovations are making a difference, it is becoming clear they aren't enough to prevent the crisis on their own. There are several reasons for this. First, history tells us that solving problems takes idealism, determination, and political will, as well as the technology to fix what's wrong. So unless we can imagine a better world, have the fortitude to act, and leaders to steer the way, it is unlikely we will succeed. Second, technological solutions often have unanticipated consequences. They solve one problem only to cause others. For instance, although drinking water chlorination has saved countless lives, it increases the risk of cancer. Similarly, although the construction of taller smokestacks has reduced local air pollution, it distributes pollutants over much larger areas, leading to more widespread contamination.

The third and most important reason why technology alone cannot solve the global eco-social crisis is that the problems we face are not just technological problems. Fundamentally, they are human problems and their roots lie in our core beliefs about our relationship with the environment—especially beliefs that we are the most important species and have the right to exploit all others and the earth itself. Only when we understand that we are all part of the web of life, and act accordingly, will we be able to avert disaster. Technological advances may buy us some time and slow down the process of decline, but they will not stop it unless we recognize the simple truth of our dependence on the earth and each other, and change our ways.

As it becomes obvious that we cannot count on technology to avert disaster, people's hopelessness is likely to intensify. But the more hopeless we become, the more likely it is that all the predictions of ecological disaster will come true. Hopelessness leads to paralysis and inaction, guaranteeing that things will continue to get worse. To stop this downward spiral, we urgently need to uncover a realistic sense of hope and find ways to nurture it. Indeed, I believe this is one of the most important tasks of our time.

Uncovering and nurturing a realistic sense of hope is very challenging because it means we must stay open to both the unthinkable—a future that seems too terrifying to contemplate—and what may be impossible—preventing global eco-social disaster. Even though navigating a course between this Scylla and Charybdis is extremely daunting, I believe it can be done. By having the courage to face our fears, we can move forward. By being willing to let go of our expectations and beliefs, we can take the next step. When we understand that "the frontiers of the possible are not determined by the limits of the actual"[32] we can uncover and nurture a realistic sense of hope.

Uncovering and Nurturing Hope

This book is based on what I have learned about hope. Like my previous book, *The Rise of the U.S. Environmental Health Movement* (Rowman & Littlefield, 2013), it draws on my experience of working on environmental and related health and social issues over the past 35 years. Over that time, I have worked in several settings. In the early 1980s, I launched my career in the City of Toronto in Canada, where I established and later managed its Environmental Protection Office, the first local government environmental office in Canada. In the 1990s, I moved to Ottawa and ran a successful environmental policy consulting company, providing services to the Canadian federal government and international agencies. In 2000, I went back to school to do a masters' degree in cultural anthropology and social transformation focusing on eco-social issues, so that I could better understand how change happens in societies, organizations, and groups. Then in 2002, I moved to the Pacific Northwest to teach at Antioch University Seattle in its Center for Creative Change. I left the University in 2016.

My work has often left me feeling afraid, angry, and very, very sad. Because of this, I have thought a lot about hope. Supported by my Quaker and Buddhist faiths—yes, I am a Quaker and a Buddhist—I have studied what hope can mean in these troubled times and how it can be sustained. This book is the result.

In it, I propose the idea of "intrinsic hope." Intrinsic hope is different from conventional hope because it is not based on the expectation that life will give us what we hope for. Instead, intrinsic hope is a deep, abiding trust in whatever happens and in the human capacity to respond to it positively. It accepts life just as it is and works with it, whether or not it's what we want. As one of my students said, "It's about making the best of any situation and never, ever giving up."

In contrast, conventional hope—in this book I call it "extrinsic hope"—is based on the naïve expectation that life will give us whatever we hope for. In other words, extrinsic hope is about anticipating improvements in our external circumstances. But life doesn't always give us what we hope for, and when it doesn't we can feel disappointed, sad, and angry. Intrinsic hope does not come with this limitation because it doesn't depend on the expectation that life will conform with our wishes.

Intrinsic hope is not something we need to find or create because it is already inside us. Indeed, it is inherent in all life. We may not experience it much in everyday life because our extrinsic hopes are so strong, but it is still there and we can uncover it and nurture it whenever we want.

Based on my experience, the first step in uncovering intrinsic hope is to name our feelings about the global eco-social crisis. Paradoxically, by acknowledging our fear, disappointment, anger, frustration, guilt, sadness, despair, grief, and other similar feelings, the more hopeful we can become. Conversely, the more we ignore them, the more hopeless we will feel. So in Chapter One, I identify and explore some common feelings about the global eco-social crisis.

The second step is to develop a firm foundation for intrinsic hope that can replace the wishful thinking of extrinsic hope. Even though we are all born with intrinsic hope, we still need a rationale to keep going. So in Chapter Two, I outline ten reasons that have helped me to be hopeful. The third step, described in Chapter Three, is to understand the nature of intrinsic and extrinsic hope in more detail.

The second part of this book examines how intrinsic hope can be nurtured. Over my career, I have thought a lot about this and Chapters Four to Nine outline what I have learned so far. In these chapters, I propose six "habits of hope"—intentional practices that have helped me foster intrinsic hope. They are: being present, expressing gratitude, loving the world, accepting what is, taking action, and persevering for the long haul. I have dedicated a chapter to each of these topics and at the end of each one I include a few suggestions about how to nurture the habit in a text box called "Try This." To wrap up the book, I have written a short concluding chapter that draws on the myth of Pandora's box. Although she is widely blamed for releasing pain, suffering, and evil into the world, could it be that Pandora also gave us the gift of intrinsic hope?

Although this book focuses on the global eco-social crisis, the ideas in it can be applied to anything. We all have extrinsic hopes and feel disappointment, sadness, and anger when we don't get what we hope for, and we can all uncover and nurture intrinsic hope as a constructive alternative. So I encourage you not to limit your thinking about hope to the unfolding crisis, but to see it more broadly in the context of your entire life.

Although intrinsic and extrinsic hope may be new phrases, they are ways of thinking that have been around for millennia. Today, they can help us respond positively to the global eco-social crisis, just as they have helped humankind respond to death, disasters, and tragedies through the ages. It seems that the best wisdom for facing the global eco-social crisis is no different than the best wisdom for facing any other type of personal or collective crisis.

Uncovering and nurturing intrinsic hope is a journey that is both challenging and inspiring. It helps us to look at our fears about the future and enables us to keep going no matter what happens. It challenges our assumptions about ourselves and what we believe is possible. And it gives us a reason to live at a time of gathering darkness. Most of all, uncovering and nurturing intrinsic hope is an ongoing journey. It is not somewhere we arrive or something we can get and keep. Uncovering and nurturing intrinsic hope requires ongoing effort because it is constantly eroded by the harm that human beings continue to inflict on the environment and on each other. Indeed, as the global eco-social crisis worsens, I believe that the need for intrinsic hope will increase. With this in mind, I sincerely "hope" that you find this book useful. May it restore your hope and help you to live courageously in these troubled times.

Uncovering Intrinsic Hope

CHAPTER 1

Naming Our Feelings about the Global Eco-social Crisis

> *Naming things, breaking through taboos and denial is the most dangerous, terrifying and crucial work. This has to happen in spite of political climates or coercions, in spite of careers being won or lost, in spite of the fear of being criticized, outcast or disliked. I believe freedom begins with naming things. Humanity is preserved by it.*
>
> — EVE ENSLER, *The Power and Mystery of Naming Things*

NAMING OUR FEELINGS about the global eco-social crisis is the first step in uncovering intrinsic hope because if we do not name them, we can't do anything about them. It's similar to psychotherapy. As anyone who has ever been in therapy knows, you start by talking about what's bothering you. Only then can you understand yourself and work with your situation. This is because identifying our feelings decreases the emotional charge that accompanies them. In other words, to name our feelings is to tame them.

Furthermore, when we express our feelings about the state of the world to others, we create the space for them to talk about theirs. We make it OK for them to open up to us. And when this happens, we often realize our feelings are similar and that we are not alone. This is very comforting and supportive. Sharing our feelings with others can also be a powerful political act. For example, the women's movement of the 1970s and 1980s was born when women got together in consciousness-raising groups to talk about their shared experiences of discrimination. From these meetings, they developed and launched a program of social action. As social activist Starhawk says, "When we express our feelings... the fog rolls away.... We can take action to hold accountable those who have and do hurt us."[1]

Naming and expressing our feelings about what's happening takes courage because it requires facing some distressing emotions. Indeed, one of my friends who reviewed a draft of this chapter suggested that I put a warning sign at the beginning because it discusses feelings that can be difficult to talk about. However, this is the only truly hopeful way forward because ignoring painful feelings doesn't make them go away, as I mentioned in the Introduction.

Sometimes it is challenging to find the right words because emotions resist being put into rigid verbal shapes. They are often impossible to pin down and refuse to be contained, spilling over the edges of vocabulary into formless and ill-defined puddles on the floor. This problem is exacerbated by the fact that there have not been any words to describe feelings associated with the global eco-social crisis until recently. Only now are psychologists and linguists beginning to fill this etymological void by creating phrases such as solastalgia (the distress caused by environmental change), environmental melancholia, eco-angst, and ecosystem distress syndrome. But naming them is essential to uncover a realistic sense of hope. So here are some of mine, as best as I can express them:

The first and most predominant one is an intense panicky fear that we will not succeed in preventing the crisis and that the earth will become barren and inhospitable to life. This is accompanied by unpleasant bodily sensations, including a rapid heart rate, shortness of breath, clamminess, and nausea. I also feel constriction and tightness throughout my body, as if something was gripping me from the inside.

Also, at an emotional level, I feel profound disappointment about how little has been done so far, despite all the promises made by governments, international agencies, and corporations. This is usually followed by self-righteous anger and frustration directed at the same governments, international agencies, and corporations. Then I often feel some shame and guilt about my personal lifestyle and that I am not doing enough to stop the crisis. In addition to these feelings are profound sadness, despair, and, most of all, grief. Most often, they all come together, feeding off each other and making me feel hopeless about the future. I try to see them as Thich Nhat Hanh's bells of mindfulness—life's way of waking me up to the reality of the mess we're in.

Now that I have revealed my feelings, I invite you to take a few minutes to tune into yours. So put down this book for a moment close your eyes, and relax. Take three deep breaths and ask yourself what you feel about the state of the world. As you reflect on this question, notice what feelings come up in your mind and what sensations arise in your body. Try to observe them and let them be. Try not to get caught up in following them, judging them, or pushing them away. Just hold them gently and lovingly in your heart. Then without forcing anything, try to name them. Writing them down can help. This exercise can be difficult but I encourage you to try it. If you feel overwhelmed and can't stay with your feelings, please don't worry. This is quite normal. Just let yourself experience whatever comes up and be with it in your heart.

When I think about what's happening I often feel as if I am drowning in a tsunami of emotions. I feel overwhelmed, helpless, and defeated, and I usually react in one of two ways. Either I try to deny or minimize what is happening, or I fall into apathy and do nothing at all. Denial and apathy about our situation are quite normal, just like the other feelings I have mentioned. But they are a bit different because they serve to protect us from emotional overload and breakdown. In other words, sometimes the bells of mindfulness are so deafening that we need some ear protection. By helping us to hold ourselves together in tough times, denial and apathy enable us to cope with too many destabilizing emotions. In the short term, these coping mechanisms are essential, but in the long term they don't serve us well.

Your feelings may not be exactly the same as mine, but chances are they are similar. So let's take a look at them in more detail.

Fear

As much as we try to avoid it, fear is one of the most common feelings. Looking back, I can see how much it has dominated my life. Growing up in the 1960s, I remember being terrified about nuclear war. I believed that everyone and everything I loved would be destroyed in an instant, including me. Then as a teenager in the 1970s, I read Rachel Carson's book *Silent Spring* and became frightened about the dangers of toxic chemicals. Then in the late 1990s and early 2000s, I became deeply alarmed about climate disruption and its consequences. Today, all of these fears, as well as others, still live in me.

Fear is not all bad, however. It can be a motivating force and rouse us out of complacency. It's only when it drags us down and we can't see a way forward that it becomes unhealthy and debilitating. When fear becomes an overwhelming and paralyzing state of dread, it controls our thoughts and emotions and prevents us from taking action.

One day, when I felt curious and courageous, I decided to name my fears about the state of the world. This is what I wrote:

I am afraid of the future. I am afraid about what we are leaving to our children and all future generations. I am afraid there will not be enough food and water to support human beings, let alone other species. I am afraid the earth will overheat and increasingly severe weather will make life difficult or impossible for billions of people, especially the poor and vulnerable. I am afraid of the wars, violence, and civil unrest that will be triggered by resource scarcity and by the millions of environmental refugees who will be looking for somewhere hospitable to live. I am afraid of ever-worsening pollution and all the health problems it will cause. Most of all, I am afraid humankind has already passed the tipping point and it is too late—our species has doomed itself and countless other species to extinction or at the very least, a vastly diminished existence.

I also noticed another type of fear: the fear of acknowledging and expressing these fears. Like the first type, this one has several dimensions: I am scared that if I really acknowledge my fears, even to myself, they will engulf me. I will lose control and get mired down in hopelessness and despair. I am also afraid that if I express my fears to others, they will think I am crazy. And finally I am afraid of inflicting my fears on others because I don't want them to feel awkward or embarrassed.

This second type of fear is fed by cultural values that regard expressing fear as a sign of weakness. As children, we are taught to be optimistic, cheerful, and upbeat. To disclose we are afraid is frowned on. Fear is an extremely uncomfortable topic of conversation that is usually avoided at all costs. Like sex, money, and religion, people don't talk about their fears in polite society. It's like farting in public.

These two types of fear—fears of the global eco-social crisis and fears of expressing our fears—are a double whammy. Our fears about our fears keep us trapped in a conspiracy of silence that makes us feel even more hopeless.

There's a third type of fear I'd like to mention: economic fear. I have not experienced it personally, but I know people who have. This type of fear is widespread in towns dependent on polluting industries. Places like Hayden, Arizona, which depends on the ASARCO copper smelter, Libby, Montana, which relied on asbestos mining, and Gary, Indiana, which was built by the US Steel Corporation. In these places, employees can be afraid to speak out about pollution or hazardous working conditions because they may lose their jobs. Similarly, people in these communities can be afraid to say anything in case the company leaves town or closes down. These worries are very understandable but it is tragic when people put their fears ahead of their own health and the health of the environment.

Although staying silent about our fears does not serve us, it does serve people in positions of political and economic power—the power-holders—because it enables them to control us more easily. Think about what happened in the US after the events of 9/11. The Republican White House intentionally manufactured a climate of fear to silence dissent, so it could declare the so-called War on Terror. Although terrorism did, and still does, pose a real threat to US national security, the dangers were deliberately exaggerated so Congress could be persuaded to ride roughshod over individual rights and pass the *Homeland Security Act*. The power-holders know that fearful, silent people are easy to manipulate and control.

Disappointment

Like many people who work on environmental and social issues, I have experienced a lot of disappointments. In my twenties, my hopes that the government would shut down polluting industries and clean up toxic waste dumps were disappointed. In my thirties, my hopes for sustainable development—a concept popularized by the 1987 report *Our Common Future*[2] and the 1992 Earth Summit—were disappointed. Then in my forties and fifties, my hopes for strong and effective international action on climate disruption were disappointed.

Disappointment is what we experience when life does not conform to our wishes and our hopes are unfulfilled. We hope to stop environmental destruction, put an end to poverty, and build a just, peaceful, and sustainable world, but we're not having much success, so it's only natural to feel disappointment. It's a feeling of unhappiness, dissatisfaction, and displeasure all rolled into one. It is a setback, a bummer, and a letdown. And it often leads to some of the other feelings I describe later in this chapter, especially self-righteous anger, frustration, sadness, despair, and grief.

Over the years, I have found it helpful to acknowledge my disappointment and put it in a larger perspective. I try to remember that whatever I am feeling disappointed about probably isn't the end of the world—even if it is a step closer to it. I also try to remember to feel grateful for all the gifts of life I have received. These things help.

Self-Righteous Anger and Frustration

Of all my feelings about the global eco-social crisis, my self-righteous anger and frustration bother me most. I do not consider myself an aggressive person, but I get mad when I hear about corporate greed, political dishonesty, starving children, or the latest environmental "accident." Politicians who deny climate disruption drive me especially crazy. In these moments, I become a different person. Although I rarely get angry in public, my internal frustration boils over and I want to strike out against those I identify as the enemy. In an instant, I have acted as prosecutor, judge, and jury and forever condemned those I consider guilty.

As just one example, a few years ago, I got very angry at then Canadian Prime Minister Stephen Harper because his Conservative government weakened or eliminated many of the policies and programs I had worked on in the 1990s. During that time, I helped to strengthen the *Canadian Environmental Assessment Act*, the *Fisheries Act*, the *Canadian Environmental Protection Act*, and the *Species at Risk Act*. This legislation improved environmental protection in Canada and I felt a sense of pride at having been involved. Imagine my fury when these acts were systemically dismantled in the name of economic growth. Over the time he was

Prime Minister (2006–15), Harper took all these environmental protections apart by removing safeguards, diluting enforcement, siding with corporate polluters, and withdrawing from international agreements. He even destroyed a lot of historical environmental information.

Like me, many people are angry and frustrated about what is happening. They are justifiably upset. It all seems so black and white. We are the good guys and "they"—whoever they are—are the bad guys. We have God and the angels on our side and "they" are the devil incarnate. There is no middle ground because self-righteous anger offers the clarity of a simple dualism—right or wrong. It comes with thoughts of outrage and indignation that say, "I'm better than you because I'm right and you're a bad person because you are wrong." In doing so, it sets a moral standard and then judges everyone by it. Claiming the high ground, self-righteous anger makes itself superior, and everyone else, especially polluters and politicians, inferior.

Self-righteous anger and frustration blame others for whatever we think is wrong. But in doing so they confuse the accused's actions with their identity. They conflate the doer with the deed and fail to recognize that everyone is more than what they do or say. Do you define yourself solely in terms of your actions? Probably not. Let's look at it another way. If I watch a TV show and I don't like it, I don't get angry at the TV. It simply aired the show. Similarly, we don't have to get angry or frustrated at people when they behave a certain way, even if we believe their actions are wrong. In other words, we can respect everyone, whether we like their behavior or not. Mohandas Gandhi was an expert at this. He was unfailingly courteous and polite to the British overlords who ruled India, at the same time as he opposed their oppressive policies and struggled for his country's independence. Although Gandhi was outraged about the unjust political and economic systems imposed by the British, his anger and frustration were not self-righteous or directed at individuals.

So why do we get so angry and frustrated?

Most importantly, anger and frustration make us feel good about ourselves. Righteousness and goodness are very closely allied with each other, so we think that if we are right we will automatically be good. And we all want to be good, don't we? In this way, righteousness and goodness say it's OK to feel angry or frustrated at someone because they are bad or wrong and we are good and right.

But self-righteous anger inevitably alienates the objects of its rage and make them angry at us. As well, it can be a big turn-off for people who are not sure where they stand on an issue, because they think they could be judged next. I know I have felt judged by self-righteous activists on many occasions. In these ways, self-righteous anger and frustration shut down the possibility of constructive dialogue and prevent the peaceful resolution of differences. As one of my colleagues used to ask our students, "Do you want to be right or do you want to be effective?" This is an interesting question to consider.

That said, anger and frustration at the global eco-social crisis can be helpful if they are not self-righteous or directed at individuals. By uniting people against a common cause, they can motivate social change. Priest and social activist William Sloane Coffin put it this way, "A capacity for anger is very important because if you don't have anger, you will begin to tolerate the intolerable...If you are not angry, you are probably a cynic. And if you lower your quotient of anger at oppression, you will lower your quotient of compassion for the oppressed. I see anger and love as very related."[3] So by all means, hold onto your anger and frustration, but please make sure they are not self-righteous.

Shame and Guilt

When I think about the global eco-social crisis, I often feel shame and guilt. I know my lifestyle contributes to it and I feel I am not doing enough to stop it. I eat food that has been transported thousands of miles to reach my dinner plate, drive a car, and occasionally travel by airplane. Even though I try to live modestly by North American standards, my ecological footprint is far greater than the earth's capacity to support me. My lifestyle and the lifestyles of more than a billion other affluent people mean that future generations will not have the same opportunities that I enjoy.

Intellectually, I know that some people bear much more responsibility than I do. Ordinary folks like you and me may be complicit, but the power-holders got us into this mess. They created and maintain the political and economic systems that are destroying the planet; the public is mostly an unwitting participant. But despite this, I still feel that whatever I do isn't enough.

A while ago, I taught a student who had served two tours as a combat medic in Iraq, providing front-line care to horribly wounded and dying soldiers. His descriptions of what he had witnessed were graphic and profoundly disturbing. Not surprisingly, he was diagnosed with PTSD and eventually discharged. When I knew him, he was still suffering from PTSD but his guilt and shame troubled him much more.

He felt guilty and ashamed because he had participated in a war which he believed was based on America's desire to control Iraqi oil and had nothing to do with terrorism. In tears, he told me about the poverty, hunger, and child labor he had seen while he was driving around in a heated Humvee, with food in his stomach, warm clothes on his back, and the knowledge that his family was safe at home. He could not live with the awareness that he was participating in a war to satisfy America's addiction to oil—a war that was killing many innocent Iraqi citizens and would likely rob them of their natural resources. Thankfully, with counseling and support, he has since been able to come to terms with his feelings.

Shame (the feeling that I am a bad person) and guilt (the feeling that I have harmed others) are similar to anger because they are about blame. The difference is that when we are angry, we blame others and when we feel shame or guilt we blame ourselves. Shame and guilt are self-inflicted wounds that makes us feel like failures—no-good, worthless people who ought to do better. They tell us that we don't deserve joy, happiness, or anything positive in our lives and they are a guarantee of hopelessness.

Unlike shame, guilt can be a useful emotion because it can help us take responsibility for our actions and change our behavior. But it can also make us take too much responsibility. This is unhelpful for two reasons. First, although guilt can lead to positive change, too much of it can lead to apathy. If we feel personally responsible for the entire crisis, we will probably feel disheartened and depressed. Second, taking too much responsibility can take it away from those who are more responsible than we are. If we feel guilty about things we cannot control, we allow those who are responsible to avoid taking ownership for their actions. This is why the power-holders want ordinary people to feel guilty about our environmental and social problems. The more they can make us feel bad about them, the less responsibility they have to take. So although ordinary folks bear some responsibility, it is important to put the majority of it where it belongs—on the shoulders of the power-holders.

If we can get clear about what is our responsibility and what is not, we can begin to work with our feelings and decide what to do about them. For instance, if you feel guilty about your contribution to climate disruption, you can take public transit whenever you can, buy a hybrid/electric car, limit the number of airplane flights you take, or become a vegetarian. Although these actions may not make you feel entirely guiltless or shame-free, they will help.

Sadness and Despair

I feel tremendous sadness and despair about the global eco-social crisis. To me, these two feelings are on a continuum. At one extreme, there is an aching sadness about the harm humankind is inflicting on the earth and each other and, at the other, there is the pain of complete despair. The difference is that when you feel sad, there's still a little hope left. But when you despair, you don't have any hope at all. Indeed, "despair" comes from the Latin *de-sperare*, meaning to be without hope.

If you experience sadness and despair, I encourage you to pause and reflect on where you are on this continuum right now. Just as I invited you to tune into your feelings about the state of the world earlier in this chapter, now I invite you to look specifically at your sadness and despair. So take three deep breaths and then check in with yourself. What is the predominant feeling in your heart in this moment? Is it sadness or despair or a combination? Where are you on the continuum? You could try to rate your feelings on a one-to-ten scale, with one being a subtle sadness and ten being complete despair.

Most of the time, I live with moderate sadness—somewhere between a three and a four. But I have experienced complete despair. One of my worst bouts was when I was working for the City of Toronto in the early 1980s. One gloomy fall day, I was on a tour of the leaking toxic waste dump in Love Canal, New York, with government officials from Canada and the US. By then, all the residents had been evacuated and there was a high chainlink fence surrounding the site with large red warning signs every hundred yards proclaiming: "DANGER: HAZARDOUS WASTE AREA. UNAUTHORIZED PERSONNEL KEEP OUT." in bold red and black capital letters.

Looking through the fence I could see rows of boarded-up houses and empty streets. The silence was palpable and I felt overwhelmed as I looked at the poisoned ground. The knowledge that children were the most seriously affected, with reports of seizures, learning problems, skin rashes, and hyperactivity, as well as birth defects and miscarriages, became too much to bear. Furthermore, I knew that Love Canal was only one of hundreds of abandoned dump sites in the area, many of which were leaking toxic chemicals and polluting the Niagara River and Lake Ontario—the source of drinking water for about 40 million Americans and Canadians. Despair engulfed me.

Environmental sadness and despair are different from the personal sadness and despair people feel during difficult periods in their lives. Personal sadness and despair are usually connected with specific events, so they often dissipate over time. But environmental sadness and despair don't go away because humankind continues to harm the environment. In addition, they are less about what is happening to us as individuals and more about what is happening to the entire planet. These two factors—their persistence and their scale—make environmental sadness and despair more challenging than personal sadness and despair.

Environmental sadness is not as overwhelming as environmental despair. When we experience sadness, we may be able to detach ourselves sufficiently to explore it. The emotional heaviness of despair makes this more difficult, as I found at Love Canal. So I recommend working with environmental sadness first. In my experience, it always has something to teach me, if I am willing to learn. By holding it gently in my heart and inquiring into its causes, I have learned about my environmental values and ideals, my sense of connection to other people, and, most of all, my love for the earth.

Working with environmental despair is more challenging because it is an overpowering emotion. Deep despair refutes any possibility that our situation is workable or may improve. To work with despair, I find it necessary to be extremely patient and tender with myself, spend time in a healing environment, and surround myself with loving and supportive friends.

Grief

When I think about my environmental grief, there are several types, including:

1. Grief for what we know has been lost. I grieve for the mammoths, passenger pigeons, auks, and all the other species we

know humankind has driven to extinction. I grieve for old-growth forests that have been deliberately cut down, I grieve the loss of clean air and water, and I grieve for the loss of the natural landscapes of my childhood that have been built on or paved over.

2. Grief for what we do not know has been lost. Although we know some of what humankind has destroyed, we do not know the full consequences of our actions. I grieve for the things we have lost without anyone knowing or caring. I grieve for our species' ignorance and lack of awareness.

3. Grief for what future generations will have lost. I grieve for what our children and their children will have lost. They will never see a Tasmanian tiger, a golden toad, a Caribbean monk seal, or a Pyrenean ibex—all species that have gone extinct in the past 30 years. They will never see the full majesty of the world's glaciers or the complete size of the Aral Sea. They will never see many wondrous things that my generation has been privileged to see.

Scientists can document these and other losses, but grief about the destruction of life on earth cannot be described with facts and figures alone. It's a different kind of knowing—a knowing that goes beyond the rational mind and lives in the heart. Environmental grief always comes as a shock, even when it is anticipated. Suddenly we realize that something has been irreparably damaged or doesn't exist anymore, and this creates a distressing void in our lives. Moreover, like environmental sadness and despair, environmental grief is on a much larger scale than personal grief, because it is about what we have lost collectively and because human beings continue to destroy the earth. As long as humankind carries on its ecocidal rampage, people will continue to experience environmental grief.

What makes it worse is that this type of grief is not culturally accepted or acknowledged, so there aren't any social support systems to help. Unlike the grief counseling and therapy available to those mourning the death of a loved one, there are no systems in place for those grieving the death of life on earth, unless you happen to come across the work of Joanna Macy and others like her.

This may be because environmental grief is a relatively new phenomenon. Naturalist Aldo Leopold was one of the first people to describe it. He wrote: "For one species to mourn the death of another is a new thing under the sun." He goes on: "The Cro-Magnon who slew the last mammoth thought only of steaks. The sportsman who shot the last (passenger) pigeon thought only of his own prowess. The sailor who clubbed the last auk thought of nothing at all."[4] In other words, they were completely unaware of what they were losing so they did not grieve it. In contrast, we know what we are doing and this knowledge causes untold and immeasurable grief.

But there's something else about environmental destruction that intensifies the grief I experience—the awareness of so much loss reminds me of my own death. Whenever I reflect on the demise of a species, a landscape, or a way of life, I feel afraid of my mortality. In this way, the global eco-social crisis isn't just something scary happening in the external world, it evokes a deep-seated and visceral dread of my personal death. You might consider if this is true for you too.

There are two small islands of solace in my ocean of environmental grief. The first is that grief understands that something has gone and can never be fully restored. It recognizes that this is not what we wanted or what we planned, but it is what we have. Although very painful, this awareness is the beginning of acceptance (see Chapter Seven). Although I don't believe it is possible to completely accept the scale of environmental death and loss, we can begin to accept our feelings about it. The second is the realization that death and loss are necessary for life. Without them, the new cannot be born. So however much grief we feel, death and loss open up the possibility of creation. Just as the phoenix rises from the ashes, perhaps we can make meaning of our environmental grief by working to give birth to a just, peaceful, and sustainable world.

Now that I have named and explored some of my feelings about the global eco-social crisis, I'd like to look at the emotions that come up when these feelings overwhelm me and it all feels too much. For me, these secondary feelings include denial and apathy.

Denial and Apathy

Sometimes when I feel overwhelmed by my feelings about the global eco-social crisis, I want to deny what's happening. I want to shout out, "This cannot be true" or, "I don't believe it." In this way, denial tries to refute reality. Wanting to improve my understanding, I made a list of some different types of denial I have experienced or seen in others.

1. Denying the scientific facts. This is the most obvious form of denial and it's easiest to see in those who refute climate disruption. Some reject that it's happening and others don't believe it is caused by human actions. In 2016, 12 percent of Americans did not believe in global warming and 32 percent blamed naturally occurring changes in the atmosphere.[5] This, despite the fact that more than 99 percent of climate scientists agree that climate disruption is real and more than 97 percent agree that human beings are causing it.[6] Although there has never been a stronger scientific consensus about an environmental problem, many still deny the scientific facts.

2. Denying personal experiences of the global eco-social crisis. Sometimes, victims of floods, droughts, hurricanes, and severe storms don't want to blame climate disruption or accept it is real.[7] They regard extreme weather events as isolated, freak occurrences rather than part of a larger pattern. Why don't they make the connections? Perhaps it's too scary to admit we are facing a global catastrophe. Unless people have the emotional

and psychological equipment to hold such a terrifying prospect in their minds, they resort to denying their own experience.

3. Denying the seriousness of the situation. Even if people do not deny the science or their own experience, some refuse to accept the gravity of the situation. This type of denial believes that everything will somehow be OK. Technology or God will save us.
4. Denying the global eco-social crisis could affect one's personal health and wellbeing. Some acknowledge what's happening but deny it could affect them. For instance, 58 percent of Americans believe that global warming will affect people in the US, but only 40 percent think it will harm them personally.[8]
5. Denying any personal responsibility whatsoever. This type of denial passes the buck to someone else, who can then pass it onto others. It is the opposite of taking too much responsibility. There is always someone else to blame—the government, corporations, our neighbors. But the truth is we all share responsibility even though some are more accountable than others.
6. Denying that positive change is possible. This type of denial acknowledges there is an unprecedented crisis but it refuses to believe that we can do anything about it. It is deeply pessimistic and predicts failure for any positive or constructive actions. This is the most dangerous type of denial because it is a self-fulfilling prophecy.

After I wrote this list, I could better understand why some people are in complete denial of the global eco-social crisis and I'd like to think that this has made me more compassionate towards them.

Other times that I feel overwhelmed by my feelings, I experience apathy. I want to roll up into a ball with a blanket over my head and do nothing. I feel lethargic and lazy. I can't be bothered. Unlike denial, apathy is passive and seems to be a lack of concern or indifference. But when I looked at it more carefully, I realized it isn't about not having any feelings; it's about being overwhelmed by too many and not being able to cope. Apathy says, "It's all too much," "I don't want to feel anything," and "I feel helpless." Similar to psychic numbing[9] apathy is a natural tendency to dissociate from a painful reality when life is too overwhelming. As T. S. Eliot said "Humankind cannot bear very much reality."[10] But bear it, we must.

Concluding Thoughts

In this chapter, I have named and expressed my feelings about the global eco-social crisis and encouraged you to do the same. In my experience, this is very empowering work because we discover pieces of ourselves that we have previously avoided or ignored. Identifying them restores parts of our humanity, making us whole. For me, it was as if I recovered my heart. However, it can be uncomfortable and a bit scary at first. So please be gentle with yourself. Don't push or force yourself to describe your feelings. Instead, just invite them into your mind and hold them for as long as you can. Eventually they will name themselves.

This chapter may have been difficult for you to read. It was certainly difficult for me to write. It brought me face-to-face with my own feelings about the state of the world and made me look at how I try to ignore them. As I tried to understand my own fears, disappointment, anger, frustration, guilt, shame, sadness, despair, and grief, as well as my denial and apathy, I became even more aware of the need to have a solid foundation for hope. And this is the subject of the next chapter.

CHAPTER 2

Reasons for Hope

> *Always be prepared to give an answer*
> *to everyone who asks you to give the reason*
> *for the hope that you have.*
> — 1 Peter 3:15

IN THIS ERA OF ECO-SOCIAL CRISIS, it is essential to base our hope on solid ground rather than wishful thinking or naïve optimism. Indeed, as environmental conditions continue to deteriorate and hopelessness becomes more widespread, the need for a rationale is likely to increase. So what possible reasons are there for hope today? In this chapter, I propose ten.

Life Is Inherently Hopeful

The most important reason is that life is inherently hopeful. To quote Cicero: "While there is life, there is hope." If ever there was a reason for hope, it is that life is constantly being recreated and reborn. Birth always follows death. Day always follows night. Spring always follows winter. The cycle of life has gone on for time immemorial and will continue to do so. Despite meteorites, volcanic eruptions, earthquakes, ice ages, heat waves, and mass extinctions, life has continued to survive and flourish. And even if some idiot drops a nuclear bomb or runaway climate disruption becomes a reality, life will go on with or without humankind. Life is inherently hopeful and this is the greatest single reason for hope. To live is to hope and to be hopeful is to be in harmony with life.

I find the natural world is a profound source of hope. It has an enduring quality and yet is always changing. As I write these words, I am looking out of my office window onto the water of Puget Sound. Some days it appears grey and flat, on others blue and sparkling, and sometimes whitecaps resemble the snow-covered Cascade mountains in the distance. Then there are the patterns on the surface. Created by tides, winds, subtle variations in water temperature, and the occasional passing boat or whale, they too are always in flux. But despite the water's ever-changing appearance, there is also something timeless about it. And this never-ending experience of change and changelessness gives me hope.

Even when it is not especially beautiful, nature can be a source of hope. One day in late 2015, the President of Antioch University Seattle told me and my colleagues that our program, the Center for Creative Change, was being closed down. Not surprisingly, I felt deeply shocked, angry, and very sad, so I took a walk to process my feelings. The campus was located close to a small, poorly maintained downtown park frequented by alcoholics, drug dealers, and local dog owners. As I picked my way through the trash, broken bottles, discarded syringes, and animal waste, I noticed some bedraggled sparrows pecking at the bare earth where grass had once grown. Their loud nonstop chirping was clearly audible above the traffic noise. As I looked at them, a thought came into my mind: "If these sparrows can find something to sing about, so can I." And this gave me hope.

Nature's positivity and persistence in the face of adversity is an amazing source of hope. It's as if living beings try harder when their existence is a struggle or survival is in doubt. A dandelion sprouts between the cracks in a downtown sidewalk, even if there's no soil, little sunlight or water, lots of pollution, and a constant onslaught of passing pedestrians and dogs. A single maple tree releases hundreds of thousands of seeds, oblivious of whether any will take root and grow. Pacific salmon, heavy with eggs, strain to swim up their natal rivers and streams to spawn even though they will die in the effort. That's real hope. In fact, one might say that hope is life's love for itself.

We Know More Than Ever Before

A second reason for hope is that we know more about the environment and the damage caused by humankind than ever before. And the more information we have, the more likely we are to change our destructive habits. When I launched my career in the early 1980s, very little was known about climate disruption, toxic chemicals, and species extinction compared to what is known today. According to the National Institutes for Environmental Information, about 24 petabytes (a petabyte is a million gigabytes) of information was archived in 2015, compared with about 1 petabyte in 2000.[1] These days, scientists and researchers are studying everything from the micro to the macro and as a result we know more about the earth's atmosphere, waters, land, and living species than previous generations could have imagined possible.

This is very good news because scientific information can result in social change. Although it is rarely enough on its own, the more information we have the more likely we are to do something. For example, DDT was banned in the US only because there was strong scientific evidence that it threatened the survival of bald eagles and other raptors. Similarly, without overwhelming evidence that emissions of carbon dioxide and other greenhouse gasses cause climate disruption, it is unlikely that the Paris Agreement on climate change would have been reached. Scientific information may not be sufficient on its own to motivate change, but it is necessary.

The Future Is Uncertain

Although we know more about the environment than ever before, we do not know exactly what will happen in the future. Although things look bad, no one can be completely, one hundred percent sure what's in store. And this is a third reason for hope. Even if scientists think they know everything, nature often throws in a wild card. Prediction is not certainty and something unexpected or unanticipated often happens. That's how complex systems, like the earth, work. Their behavior is inherently chaotic and unpredictable. A butterfly flaps its wings in Brazil and there's a tornado in Texas.

Uncertainty about the future is a reason for hope because it can whisper possibility as well as danger in our ears. With so many scary predictions about the future, it's easy to feel afraid. But if you think about it, fear is usually about all the dreadful things we assume will happen, rather than about the uncertainty itself. On its own, uncertainty can contain delightful possibilities as well as terrifying dangers. It all depends what we project onto the future. If we think uncertainty means danger then we will be fearful, but if we think it means possibilities then we will be excited. Unlike certainty, uncertainty does not know what will happen.

Here's why this is important. If we were completely certain we would succeed in stopping the global eco-social crisis, we would become complacent and lack sufficient motivation because we would be so confident of success. Similarly, if we were completely certain we would fail, there would be no reason to do anything because we would believe that it's already too late. In either case, the result is the same. Inadequate action. Uncertainty is a reason for hope because it forces us to take a step into the unknown and do something. It says, "We don't know for sure what will happen, so why not try?" There is no script, score, or map for these times, hence, the best way to predict the future is to help create it.

I'm no daredevil, but I love whitewater rafting. I find it exhilarating and scary at the same time. In particular, I love approaching rapids because you never know what's going to happen. The situation is very uncertain. You hear the roar of the water getting louder and louder, but often you can't see ahead because either the river falls away in front of you or it changes course abruptly. The quickening current sweeps you along faster and faster, towards the unknown. Eventually, the white, frothy water looms into view. Only then can you begin to comprehend your situation. You navigate as best you can, but the river's in charge, not you. It sweeps you along, tossing your raft this way and that. Sometimes it flips and you get thrown out and sometimes not. But whatever happens the experience is truly awesome.

Perhaps the increasing rate of eco-social change sweeping us forward indicates that we are getting closer to the rapids. Perhaps we are starting to glimpse our situation and appreciate its risks and even its opportunities. By navigating the best we can and accepting that we cannot control everything in life, we may survive. Just like the whitewater, these times can be seen as exhilarating as well as scary and this is a source of hope.

It may be helpful to consider the different types of uncertainty we face, including:

+ uncertainty about how and when the environment will change
+ uncertainty about how and when humankind will change
+ uncertainty about the consequences of human actions.

Let's look at each of these in turn. Even though scientists are much better at forecasting the future than they used to be, they do not always get it right because they can't know everything. No one predicted the extremely rapid recovery of bald eagles in the US after DDT was banned in 1972. In 1963, there were only 417 nesting pairs in the lower 48 states but by 2006 this number had increased to almost 10,000 nesting pairs.[2] Similarly, no one predicted the rapid rate at which New England's forests have expanded and reclaimed abandoned farms and countryside. In the mid-1800s, only 30–40 percent of the land was forested, but that's now increased to about 80 percent—a recovery that naturalist Henry David Thoreau thought impossible.[3] These and other examples reveal that nature can heal from human-inflicted harm much faster than we think possible.

Of course, the opposite can be true too. For example, the climate crisis seems to be worsening faster than scientists predicted. But even so, we rarely know exactly when or how things will unfold. For instance, scientists believe that the western Antarctic ice sheet will collapse but they do not know precisely when or how. It could be months, years, or even decades. It could go all at once or piece by piece. And not knowing when or how something will happen can engender a sense of urgency that we might otherwise lack.

Then there's uncertainty about how and when humankind will change in response to the growing crisis. We just don't know. Sometimes, social change happens unexpectedly fast and other times it doesn't. Although social change on the environment can seem slower than a melting glacier, change on other issues has been surprisingly rapid. A decade ago, who would have thought that the US Supreme Court would rule in favor of marriage equality? Who would have thought that so many states would have legalized marijuana? In other words, it's not always possible to predict how or when society will change and this is a reason for hope.

The third type of uncertainty is not knowing the full consequences of human actions. We can make predictions but they are unlikely to be completely accurate. For instance, environmental impact statements attempt to predict the effects of planned development projects, however hindsight reveals they often contain over-confident forecasts of "no significant environmental effects" and fail to acknowledge the level of uncertainty. When I sat on Ontario's Environmental Assessment Board, I was shocked at the confidence that engineers and scientists had in their optimistic predictions, despite huge unknowns. Later, when I was on the Canadian Environmental Assessment Research Council, I tried to develop a process to forecast the cumulative impacts of several development projects in a single region, but the uncertainties inherent in life made it impossible to do this well.

Indeed, human actions that seem to have nothing to do with the environment can have unforeseen consequences on it. One positive example of this is the creation of the demilitarized zone between North and South Korea. Created in 1953 by the armistice agreement that ended the Korean War, it has become one of Asia's most important nature preserves. This long strip of land now provides a home for many of Korea's native plants and animals, as well as numerous migratory species. For some, such as the Manchurian Crane, it has made the difference between survival and extinction.

We May Be Able to Resolve This Crisis Because We Caused It

Although the future is uncertain and unknowable, we do know that human beings caused the global eco-social crisis. It's not as if something or someone else is responsible. No. We, the human species, got ourselves into this mess. Our thoughts, beliefs, and actions made it happen. So there is a chance—just a chance—that we may be able to resolve it by changing our thoughts, beliefs, and actions. Maybe not in our lifetimes, maybe not in our children's lifetimes. But sometime. This is a further reason for hope.

I believe we can influence the future by the decisions and actions we take today. If humankind collectively decided to change its ways and then followed through with practical and effective actions, there's no doubt that we could do a lot. We created this crisis so perhaps we can put an end to it. Failure is not inevitable if we act with creativity, courage, and compassion. As one of my colleagues says, "The future is not inevitable, it is inventible!" Giving in to the belief that change is impossible is giving up. It's like throwing in the towel in the opening round or pulling out of a race because we might not win. Surely, we are made from stronger stuff.

Already, technological advances are helping to reduce reliance on fossil fuels, clean up contaminated sites and sediments, conserve water, and replace toxic chemicals with safer ones. Although they will not solve all our problems, they are part of the solution. Moreover, there are many imaginative and exciting developments in the works, such as generating electricity from the differentials in ocean temperatures, growing food in vertical gardens to conserve water and land, building tide-powered turbines, constructing no-net-impact buildings, and reducing the amount of energy used in water desalinization.

But the path will not be easy. It will take commitment and effort for the foreseeable future. The political and economic systems that created the mess we're in are massive and appear to be unchangeable. But that's exactly what the power-holders want us to think. They want ordinary people to believe that, in the words of former British Prime Minister Margaret Thatcher, "There is no alternative." People with political and economic power created these systems with their own agendas in mind, so it is not in their interests—at least their financial interests—to change them. Quite the contrary. It suits their wallets to maintain everything exactly the way it is. But change is possible! All political and economic systems are creations of the human mind and therefore can be changed.

We are an endlessly creative and resourceful species. Our ability to imagine new possibilities and adapt to different circumstances has already enabled us to spread into every ecological niche on the planet and beyond. Adversity seems to spur human ingenuity. Necessity really is the mother of invention. All we need is an awareness of the necessity for change and the determination to work on it. And as our political and economic systems continue to destroy the earth and the state of the environment worsens, I believe these two conditions will materialize.

After all, our species can achieve amazing things when we put our minds to it. For instance, in 1961 when President Kennedy announced that the US would have a man on the moon and bring him home safely by the end of the decade, no one thought this was possible. Yet, despite the odds, human innovation made it happen and astronaut Neil Armstrong became the first person to walk on the moon in July 1969. I remember watching the fuzzy TV images beamed back to earth and marveling at this human achievement. Imagine what would happen if our species decided to work together to resolve our problems. I believe we could do it—maybe not in our lifetimes but sometime. And this is a reason for hope.

Humankind Is Beginning to Think Globally

Humankind is beginning to think globally and this is another reason for hope. We are beginning to understand that the earth, all its species, and humankind are intimately connected in a vast system of relationships. We are, as Thomas Berry said, "a communion of subjects, not a collection of objects."[4]

Our species' emerging ability to think globally is perhaps most obvious in the Gaia hypothesis. Originally developed by scientist James Lovelock in the 1970s, it proposes that the earth is a single complex and interacting system and that living organisms and their inorganic surroundings have co-evolved to support life.[5] By studying the relative stability of ocean salinity, surface temperatures, and oxygen levels in the atmosphere, Lovelock came to see the earth as a vast self-regulating system that is constantly adjusting to optimize the conditions for life. In other words, he understood that the planet itself is creating the circumstances in which life can survive and flourish. Even today, this is a mindblowing idea.

A second example is the development and spread of the internet. Over the past 30 years or so, the web has completely transformed the way people communicate with each other. When I was a teenager in the late 1960s and early 1970s, it took weeks to send a letter to another country and international phone calls were an expensive luxury. Today, the internet and the digital revolution have created a worldwide human community. By 2013, more people had cell phones than toilets[6] and by 2016, more than half of the world's population had access to the web.[7] Texts, words, images, and music can now be sent around the world in the split second it takes to hit the send button on a computer or a phone. Amazing!

A third example of the emergence of global thinking is all the multilateral environmental agreements and protocols that have been signed by national governments over the past 40 years. Between 1970–74, 42 were signed but between 1990–94, this rose to almost 120, before declining to 33 in 2010–14.[8] Although they can be motivated by a desire to protect national interests, these agreements and protocols also reveal a growing understanding of global interconnectedness. As a consultant to the Canadian federal government in the 1990s, I had the privilege of working on some of them, even though I am disappointed by the lack of implementation. These and other examples of the emergence of global thinking are a reason for hope, despite the current wave of nationalism and protectionism sweeping across the US and parts of Europe.

History Tells Us Positive Social Change Is Possible

Another reason for hope is that history tells us that positive social change is possible. The past is full of examples of ordinary people coming together, standing up for themselves, and advancing positive social change in the world. Ever since Roman plebeians rose up against their masters in the fifth century BCE, social movements have been the single most powerful force for progressive social change. They work because ordinary people are the ultimate source of power in any society. Over the long term, the power-holders can only rule with the consent—explicit or implicit—of the public. When ordinary people exercise their collective muscle, change happens, even if it can take a while. As Martin Luther King Jr. said, "the arc of the moral universe…bends towards justice,"[9] and although the arc still has a lot of bending to do, social movements have achieved an enormous amount.

I did not realize how much social movements have achieved until I was in my thirties, even though I have been involved with them for as long as I can remember. When I was a small child, my mother took me on the Aldermaston Marches, held in England every Easter to protest the development of nuclear weapons. In my teens, I led my school's Amnesty International group to protest the racist policy of apartheid in South Africa. And in my early twenties, I worked for Greenpeace in the UK and internationally. But despite this lifelong immersion in social movements, I did not grasp their full significance until I witnessed the mostly nonviolent uprisings in eastern Europe that led to the fall of the Iron Curtain and the Soviet Union in the late 1980s and early 1990s. Only then did I finally understand the power of social movements. With victories such as women's suffrage, the emancipation of slaves, the abolition of child labor, better salaries and working conditions for ordinary people, women's rights, the nuclear test ban treaty, and countless others—to say nothing of their political impacts—social movements have shaped the world we live in today.

Sadly, there is very little public recognition of their victories and the positive social changes they have achieved. There are several reasons for this. First, as a society, we are so focused on the future that we rarely look back in the rear view mirror of history and appreciate how far we have come. More importantly, the power-holders don't want ordinary people to know how effective social movements can be, because it might give us ideas and lead to civil disobedience. In addition, the media rarely portrays social movements or their successes in a positive light. I know this from my personal experience. I have participated in several peaceful protests on environmental issues and have found that they are either under-reported or not reported at all. At one march on climate disruption I was among over 1,000 peaceful protestors who walked, biked, or kayaked to the oil refineries in Anacortes, Washington. The only TV coverage was a brief story that accused the kayakers of hypocrisy because their kayaks were made of plastic, and another that focused on the Native Elders who were present, ignoring the fact that most of the marchers were from mainstream society.

But here's some good news: by reflecting on the past we can learn how to advance positive change today. Although there are many factors involved in social movements' successes, some of the main ones include:

1. A critical mass of people willing to stand up and speak truth to power. People who are willing to talk about what is wrong and what it will take to change it. Speaking out in public can require great courage and personal sacrifice but all effective social movements have demonstrated this ability. By drawing attention to the gap between the society we have and the society we want, they inspire change. Martin Luther King Jr. was an expert at this. His 1963 "I Have a Dream" speech contained both an idealistic vision of a multiracial society and an incisive critique of the racism that pervaded the US at the time. The jarring dissonance created by this juxtapositioning was one of the key factors in the success of the civil rights movement.

2. Power-holders who recognize the need for change and are willing to support it, or at least not obstruct it. If those with political and economic power can accept that the systems they created need to be replaced, then positive social change can happen relatively easily and quickly. For instance, in the late 1980s and early 1990s, the fall of communism in eastern Europe took place quite suddenly and without a lot of bloodshed because many government leaders recognized the need for change and did not stand in the way.

3. A society that responds to early warning signs and is willing to make bold decisions before problems reach crisis proportions. This type of forward looking, anticipatory decision making is the opposite of our society's short-term thinking in which corporations focus on the next quarter's profits, legislators think only about the next election cycle, and ordinary people are just

trying to get by. One example of forward looking, anticipatory thinking is the precautionary principle, which states that "when an activity raises threats of harm to human health or the environment, precautionary measures should be taken even if some cause and effect relationships are not fully established scientifically."[10]

The Growing Global Citizens' Movement

Not only is positive social change possible; there is a growing global citizens' movement demanding it. Throughout the world, people are standing up for what they believe in like never before. Calling for economic, social, and environmental justice, the global citizens' movement crosses national, generational, and issue boundaries. It was born in 1999 in Seattle in opposition to the World Trade Organization and its free trade policies. Dubbed the "Battle in Seattle," this massive protest brought together social justice activists, labor unions, students, human rights groups, religious leaders, fair trade advocates, environmentalists, and many others in a new global coalition. That was just the beginning. In the following years, the anti-globalization and Occupy movements provided further evidence of a growing global citizens' movement.

The emerging worldwide climate justice movement is the latest proof of its existence. In it, environmentalists are working alongside social justice and anti-racism activists to build a worldwide network of people concerned about climate disruption and how it affects vulnerable and marginalized populations. This social movement first showed its muscle on September 21, 2014, when about 600,000 people showed up to protest climate disruption and its injustice in more than 160 countries. Since then, the climate justice movement has gone from strength to strength, organizing several more massive international marches.

Unlike the US social movements of the 1960s and 1970s, the global citizens' movement lacks any centralized authority or decision-making structures. Its distributed leadership is a source of strength because it makes the movement very flexible and adaptable to changing circumstances. It also means that the movement cannot be broken up by picking off a small number of leaders. In his 2007 book, *Blessed Unrest: How the Largest Social Movement in the World Came into Being and Why No One Saw It Coming*, Paul Hawken described the emerging global citizens' movement this way:

> This movement…is dispersed, inchoate, and fiercely independent. It has no manifesto or doctrine, no overriding authority to check with. It is taking shape in schoolrooms, farms, jungles, villages, companies, deserts, fisheries, slums—and yes, even fancy New York hotels. One of its distinctive features is that it is tentatively emerging as a global humanitarian movement arising from the bottom up. Historically social movements have arisen primarily in response to injustice, inequities, and corruption. Those woes remain legion, joined by a new condition that has no precedent: the planet has a life-threatening disease, marked by massive ecological degradation and rapid climate change.[11]

Hope Can Be Learned

Hope can be learned. I know this because I have been its student for many years. Learning mostly in the laboratory of my own life, my greatest teacher has been the global eco-social crisis itself and my responses to it. By examining my own feelings of hopelessness and despair, I have learned how to be hopeful in these troubled times. The fact that hope can be learned is excellent news because it means we have the capacity to be hopeful regardless of our circumstances.

Learning can happen at any age. Although it is easy to assume that it stops when we leave school or college, the truth is that learning can continue throughout life, up to and including the day we die. As jazz singer Eartha Kitt allegedly said, "The tombstone will be my diploma." Each age and stage of life comes with its own opportunities for learning. In kindergarten, young children learn how to share with others and play fair. Older ones learn about the world around them and the importance of relationships. Adolescents learn how to make decisions for themselves and become independent of their parents. And adults learn how to juggle the competing demands of life and decide what is most important to them. Wherever we are on life's journey, there is always plenty to learn.

Young people often have powerful hopes. They believe they can do anything. I know I did when I was young. I believed that my generation could stop pollution, abolish nuclear weapons, put an end to world hunger, and fix everything else that was wrong with the world. I was not sufficiently arrogant to think I could do it single-handedly, but I believed these dreams could be achieved in my lifetime. Fast forward 40 years and none of my hopes has been fulfilled. Because of this, I have experienced a lot of disappointment, frustration, and sadness. But over time, I have learned two things:

1. These painful feelings arise whenever life does not give me what I hope for.
2. Expecting life to conform to my hopes is not helpful or realistic.

I have also observed that older people can lose hope and become very cynical. I think of my step-father whose political and social idealism faded and gave rise to a pessimistic and contemptuous sarcasm in his later years. As he got older, his hopes faded because he had experienced so much disappointment and he did not have intrinsic hope to fall back on. Environmentalist and poet Wendell Berry, now in his eighties, wrote:

> It is hard to have hope. It is harder as you grow old,
> for hope must not depend on feeling good
> and there is the dream of loneliness at absolute midnight.

You also have withdrawn belief in the present reality
of the future, which surely will surprise us,
and hope is harder when it cannot come by prediction
any more than by wishing.[12]

It Is Our Responsibility To Be Hopeful

Another reason to be hopeful is that it is our responsibility. We
owe it to each other and we owe it to future generations. If we are
not hopeful, how can we expect others to be? If we give up, how
can we expect them to keep going? We have a responsibility to
help each other, especially when times get tough. Whenever you
are feeling hopeless, it is my responsibility to support you by being
hopeful. Similarly, whenever I feel hopeless, it is your responsibility to support me. We are all in this together and being hopeful is
a social obligation we bear for each other.

Hope, like other emotions, is infectious. Have you ever noticed
that when you walk into a room and sit down next to someone
who is feeling good, that you feel better too? It's as if their hopefulness gets transmitted to you energetically, even without words.
Similarly, if you sit next to someone who is depressed or sad, it's
easy to pick up their feelings. Just as we can sense the earth's feelings, so we can sense other people's. Our feelings are not ours
alone. They affect others. So by being willing to uncover and nurture our own intrinsic hope, we can make others feel better and
help heal the world.

As well as our responsibility to each other, we also have a responsibility to be hopeful for our children and our grandchildren.
Elders need to demonstrate a realistic and grounded sense of hope
to younger people, and as they age, younger people need to demonstrate it to those who may come after them. As a mom, sometimes
I find it difficult to be hopeful. When I talk with my son, now
28 years old, I cannot pretend that everything will be OK. Although it is my responsibility to be hopeful for him, it is also my

responsibility to be honest with him about what's happening. But if we love future generations, we cannot deprive them of hope. No, our children and grandchildren deserve more. Much more. This is why I try to model intrinsic hope.

After all, what kind of role models will we be if we get stuck in gloomy and dark thoughts about the future? How can we possibly inspire hope in our children, if we don't reveal it in our own lives? Clearly, we cannot. For these reasons, we have a responsibility to be exemplars and to say "YES!" to the future. Always.

Just Because...What Else Would We Do?

My final reason for hope is very simple: Just because...what else would we do? If you think about it, there is really no alternative. True, we could stay in bed all day and pull the blankets over our heads and pretend the world doesn't exist, but this isn't helpful to us or anyone else. Life goes on whether we choose to show up for it or not, and we really don't have much choice about showing up unless we decide to commit suicide. Living from a stance of hope is the only positive and constructive course of action.

In my own life, I often feel overwhelmed and hopeless about the global eco-social crisis. But then, I remember how much I care for nature, for other people, and for the earth, and I realize I can't give up. I realize that I am called to keep on going and to be hopeful. It is my path and my destiny. It is part of my humanity and it is what makes *Homo sapiens* such a magnificent species. As Irish playwright and poet Oliver Goldsmith said, "Our greatest glory is not in never falling, but in rising every time we fall."[13]

The impulse for hope is part of the human condition. Even in the midst of tragedy, we human beings continue to put one foot in front of the other simply because we are alive. And because we are alive, we have the same quality of hopefulness sewn into our genes as all other species. Do we give up just because the future of life looks grim? No, we do whatever we can to make it better. Giving up is simply not an option. Not in a million years. Indeed, the more dire the situation, the more we are called to be hopeful. If you ask people working on environmental and social issues what motivates them, they will almost invariably say things like, "I care too much to stand by and do nothing," and "I have no choice, what else would I do?" As poet Adrienne Rich wrote:

> My heart is moved by all I cannot save:
> So much has been destroyed
>
> I have to cast my lot with those
> who age after age, perversely,
>
> with no extraordinary power,
> reconstitute the world.[14]

I "hope" these ten reasons are helpful to you. They have given me a firm foundation for hope, despite the worsening crisis. The third and final step in uncovering intrinsic hope is to understand the nature of intrinsic and extrinsic hope in more detail.

CHAPTER 3

Intrinsic and Extrinsic Hope

> [Hope is] a state of mind, not a state of the world…it is
> a dimension of the soul; it's not essentially dependent on
> some particular observation of the world or estimate of the
> situation. Hope is not prognostication. It is an orientation
> of the spirit, an orientation of the heart; it transcends the
> world that is immediately experienced, and is anchored
> somewhere beyond its horizons.
>
> Hope, in this deep and powerful sense, is not the same as
> joy when things are going well, or the willingness to invest in
> enterprises that are obviously heading for success, but, rather,
> an ability to work for something that is good, not just because
> it stands a chance to succeed. The more unpropitious the
> situation in which we demonstrate hope, the deeper the hope is.
> Hope is definitely not the same thing as optimism. It is not the
> conviction that something will turn out well, but the certainty
> that something makes sense, regardless of how it turns out.[1]
>
> — Vaclav Havel

IN THIS QUOTE, Vaclav Havel, writer and former president of
Czechoslovakia, asserts that hope is an inner orientation to life
and does not depend on external conditions. But this is not the
way we usually think about it. Mostly, this seemingly simple

one-syllable word rolls off the tongue as a way to express a desire for particular things to happen. We say things like "I hope to feel better" or "I hope to arrive in time for dinner." Yet Vaclav Havel's words point to a very different meaning. I first came across them when I was feeling especially hopeless and they resonated with me very deeply. It didn't take long for me to realize that hope need not be contingent on anything in the external world and that I could be hopeful no matter what happens. With this new insight, I began to appreciate that hope is much more complicated than it appears. So I did what I often do when I want to investigate a new idea—I consulted the dictionary.

I discovered that hope is primarily defined as expectation and desire. The Compact Oxford Dictionary says hope is "the expectation of something desired," and the Merriam-Webster Dictionary says it is "desire with expectation of obtainment." These definitions are based on wanting something and anticipating we will get it. In other words, they are grounded in a belief that life should give us whatever we hope for. However, in addition to these meanings, both the Compact Oxford and Merriam-Webster contain secondary, archaic definitions of hope as "trust." This older and less familiar meaning is about having faith in life without the expectation of getting what we want. Close to religious hope, this type of hope has a deep, abiding trust in whatever happens and in the human capacity to respond to it constructively. It is an attitude to life that accepts the good and the bad and sees our situation—whatever it is—as workable.

These two definitions lie at the heart of what I call extrinsic and intrinsic hope. Extrinsic hope is about hoping to achieve improvements in our external circumstances. We hope to feel better or to arrive in time for dinner. We hope to stop the climate crisis, put an end to poverty, and achieve sustainability. And if our desires are not fulfilled, we get upset. This is the most common type of hope. In contrast, intrinsic hope is the internal state of mind that

Vaclav Havel describes. It is a positive attitude to life that does not depend on achieving improvements in our personal circumstances or in the world at large.

To illustrate the difference between extrinsic and intrinsic hope, imagine you are in a dense fog. You cannot see anything except the swirling mist all around you. You don't know where you are or which way to go. You hope to get out of the fog and are afraid you won't. Then you see a light in the distance and start to walk towards it but, after you have taken a few steps, it disappears and you no longer know where you are or which way to go. Your fear comes back and you feel disappointed, frustrated, and sad. Then another light appears and you start to walk towards it, but it disappears too and your feelings return. The same thing happens again and again, and each time you feel more fearful, more disappointed, more frustrated, and sadder. This is extrinsic hope.

Then you become aware of a small light inside you. In the beginning, it's just a faint glow emanating from your heart, but the more you notice it, the brighter it becomes. Gradually it becomes strong enough for you to see your own body—your arms and legs, your hands and feet—and as you focus on it, it continues to strengthen and illuminate the ground immediately around you. You take a small step. Then, as you continue to pay attention to it, this internal light gets even brighter, allowing you to take another step and then another and another. You may not get out of the fog, but your fear diminishes because the light is there to help you. Moreover, you no longer feel disappointed, frustrated, or sad because the light never goes away. Sometimes it dims or flickers, but if you stay focused on it, it always returns to support you on your journey, one step at a time. This is intrinsic hope.

In these times of eco-social crisis, this basic difference between extrinsic and intrinsic hope is crucially important because it suggests how we can live courageously no matter how bad things get. Now let's look at these two types of hope in more detail.

Extrinsic Hope

If you are anything like me, you hope to see an end to the global eco-social crisis. Or if this seems too grandiose or remote from your experience, perhaps you hope to resolve a specific environmental or social problem in your country or state. Or perhaps you are more modest and you hope to stop a new highway from being built in your neighborhood, build a homeless shelter, or achieve some other local success. This is extrinsic hope. Of course, it isn't always about environmental or social issues. We can have extrinsic hopes about anything. We can hope to win the lottery, live until we're a hundred years old, end corporate greed, or attain any other particular outcome. The point is that we all have extrinsic hopes and they are endless—there is always something else to hope for. Extrinsic hope is part of the human condition. To understand this, just think about your desires. What exactly do you hope for?

If you investigate your hopes, you may notice they often come with a belief that life will give you what you want if your hope is strong enough or if you work hard enough. We think that life will conform to our hopes if we really, really want something or if we work really, really hard to achieve it. But this type of hope can be just wishful thinking. Here's an example. When I was a child, I hoped to win a Nobel Prize. I didn't mind which one—any one would do. But as I grew up, I came to understand that this hope was naïve and unrealistic. I was not particularly smart or clever and I wasn't going to be a world leader. I realized that no matter how much I hoped for a Nobel Prize or how hard I worked for one, life probably wasn't going to give me what I wanted.

Some extrinsic hopes are self-centered, like my desire to win a Nobel Prize, and others are altruistic, such as hopes to stop the global eco-social crisis and build a better world. Altruistic hopes are regarded as more worthy or virtuous than self-centered ones, so it's even easier to believe that life should give us what we want. After all, if life is inherently good, shouldn't it comply with our well-intentioned hopes for others? But life doesn't work that way. Altruistic hopes may be extremely noble but this is no guarantee they will be fulfilled, any more than self-centered hopes.

As I explored the idea of extrinsic hope, I began to understand it better. By examining my own experiences of it, I have identified the following key features:

Whether our extrinsic hopes are self-centered or altruistic, the common denominator is a desire to achieve specific outcomes in the external world. In other words, extrinsic hope always comes with an attachment to getting what it wants. It's an emotional stickiness or charge that says "I know what I want" or "I know what's best." It can be quite strong if we feel that we or others deserve to get what we hope for. For example, I have a strong hope for more equitable income distribution in the US because I believe that people living in poverty deserve a bigger slice of the pie. Alternatively, it can be weak if the hope is just a passing fancy. But in either case, there is an expectation that life should give us the results we hope for.

The desire to achieve certain outcomes in the external world is based on a belief that we know what should happen—that the improvements we seek are the most desirable outcomes. Even if our extrinsic hopes are very worthy, this could be seen as rather arrogant. Perhaps we don't always know what's best. Perhaps life knows more than we do. After all, life is in charge, not us. For instance, in 2016 I desperately hoped to see Hillary Clinton become president and I could not imagine anything good happening if Donald Trump was elected. But in hindsight, his presidency has offered some benefits. In particular, having a wolf in wolf's clothing in the White House has provided a political clarity that had previously been obscured. This has forced a much needed re-evaluation of the progressive agenda and led to a revitalization of social activism and citizen engagement in the US. With my belief that a Clinton victory was the best result, I could not see these benefits. Although I still think Hillary

Clinton would have made a much better president, the situation is not entirely bad.

Extrinsic hope's desire for specific improvements in life is based on a dissatisfaction with the way things are in the present. It says, "This is unacceptable," and "Life should be better than this." There's a discontent and sense of inadequacy that identifies something we do not have right now and turns it into a want or a need. In this way, extrinsic hope believes that happiness depends on getting what we hope for—whether it's a particular president, an exciting vacation, or a world without poverty. We believe we will be happy if our hopes are fulfilled, and conversely we won't be happy if they aren't.

But the truth is that extrinsic hope does not make our dissatisfaction, discomfort, and distress go away. On the contrary, it makes them worse. This is because whenever we have an extrinsic hope, there is an automatic fear that we *won't* get what we want. Even if we are not consciously aware of it, fear always accompanies extrinsic hope. Author and leadership consultant Meg Wheatley recognized this when she said, "A wild ride between hope and fear is unavoidable. Fear is the necessary consequence of feeling hopeful again. Contrary to our belief that hope and fear are opposites where one trumps the other, they are a single package, bundled together as intimate, eternal partners. Hope never enters a room without fear at its side. If I hope to accomplish something, I am also afraid I will fail. You can't have one without the other."[2] However, fear is not the only unpleasant feeling associated with extrinsic hope. To see this, think about how you feel when life does not live up to your hopes and expectations, especially those about the global eco-social crisis. Chances are, you feel some or all of the emotions I described in Chapter One.

Extrinsic hope's desire for specific outcomes has another unfortunate consequence. It's so easy to get lost in its plans and fantasies about the future that we ignore what is actually happening in the present. Thich Nhat Hanh described this by saying: "When I think deeply about the nature of hope, I see something tragic. Since we cling to our hope in the future, we do not focus our energies and capabilities on the present moment. We use hope to believe something better will happen in the future, that we will arrive at peace, or the Kingdom of God. Hope becomes a kind of obstacle."[3] Relating this to our situation today, if we cling to the extrinsic hope that we will stop the crisis, we may fail to grasp its severity. And if we fail to grasp its severity, it's unlikely we will respond effectively. In this way, extrinsic hope can prevent us from understanding our situation and preclude appropriate action, thereby reducing the chances of success.

In a similar way, extrinsic hope shuts down alternatives. Because it knows what it wants, extrinsic hope is not open to other options. For example, when I hoped to win a Nobel Prize, I could not see the vast array of possibilities in my life. I was so emotionally attached to the outcome I wanted that I could not see any other future. All I could see was the lure of a Nobel Prize. It was only after I let go of the fantasy that I could grasp the opportunities right in front of me.

A final feature of extrinsic hope is its relationship with action. One might assume that its attachment to achieving specific outcomes means that this type of hope always leads to action, but this is not so. Extrinsic hope can be a passive wish without any follow-through. Sometimes people don't take action on their extrinsic hopes because there is nothing they can do—for instance, I can say, "I hope tomorrow is sunny" but there is nothing I can do to make it sunny. Other times, extrinsic hope may not lead to action even if there is something we can do. For instance, I can say, "I hope to lose weight," but I might not do anything to actually lose weight. So with extrinsic hope, action is not guaranteed. But merely hoping that everything will turn out OK is not enough. It is like sitting on the sidelines of life and wanting someone else to solve our problems or believing that we'll get lucky and everything will be fine. This is unrealistic and self-defeating. In these perilous times, we need a hope that guarantees action.

Please understand that I am not saying that extrinsic hope is bad or wrong. But I am saying it has limitations. So why does extrinsic hope have such a hold on us? What do we get out of it?

Quite a lot, actually. Extrinsic hope lets us indulge our dreams and wishes. It enables us to escape the harsh realities of life and live in a pleasant, make-believe world. It is also an easy way to appear positive and optimistic—both highly desirable character traits in the Western dominant culture. By allowing us to think we can achieve whatever we hope for, extrinsic hope offers reassurance in an uncertain world. Moreover, as the future of life on earth becomes less certain, it is likely people will increasingly cling to extrinsic hope, thereby creating a vicious cycle of hopelessness. This is because the worse the crisis becomes, the more people will desperately hope to stop it, and the more they hope to stop it, the more fearful they will become that they won't succeed. Furthermore, the more their extrinsic hopes are not fulfilled, the more people will experience disappointment, sadness, despair, and other painful feelings. With this in mind, it is not surprising that we are fast becoming a hopeless society. This is why uncovering and nurturing intrinsic hope is so important in these times.

Intrinsic Hope

Shortly after I discovered the Vaclav Havel quote at the beginning of this chapter, I met someone who embodied intrinsic hope very powerfully. She was a Roman Catholic nun who worked at a health clinic that provided free or low-cost services to people from poor and marginalized communities. She had been orphaned at a very young age and brought up in a series of temporary foster homes. She got married when she was only 19. Subsequently, she was beaten by her husband, became homeless, and fell into a life of addiction. Then in her late twenties, she became a nun. By the time I knew her, she had been working with abused, homeless, and addicted women for almost 30 years. Even though the people she was trying to help often gave up on themselves and relapsed back into their old habits, she never gave up on them. No matter what they said or did, she was always there offering them her unconditional love and support. It was obvious to me that her hope was not dependent on how the women behaved or on anything in the external world. It was intrinsic hope.

This type of hope is evident in the world's faith traditions. Because they seek to understand human experience, they have all explored it in some way. This is most easily seen in the Abrahamic religions' trust in God. In fact, some scholars refer to Judaism as the religion of hope because early Jews endured so many cataclysms and disasters. Intrinsic hope can also be seen in Christianity. In one passage from the Bible that sounds as if it is predicting climate disruption, we are told, "God is our refuge and strength, a very present help in trouble. Therefore we will not fear, though the earth be moved, and though the mountains be carried into the midst of the sea."[4] And in another, St. Paul says, "Hope does not disappoint."[5] Similarly, Islamic hope is based on trusting God unconditionally. As the Qu'ran advises, "And for everyone who places his trust in God, He [alone] is enough."[6] This type of faith in God can be seen as intrinsic hope if it is free of expectations for specific outcomes. However, it can easily become extrinsic hope if there is a belief that He (and it usually is a "he") will save us.

Eastern traditions, such as Buddhism and Hinduism, do not believe in a single all-powerful deity or savior. Instead, they have faith in the oneness and interdependence of all life. Moreover, unlike the Abrahamic religions, their hope is derived from a thorough and careful examination of the causes of suffering. Advocating that expectations and desires (aka extrinsic hope) are the root of all suffering, Buddhism and Hinduism recommend working with our minds to dispel them. Thus, they recognize that happiness and hopefulness are an inside job. The Bhagavad Gita, Hinduism's most sacred text, puts it well. In describing how the wise live, Krishna tells Arjuna: "They live in wisdom who see themselves in all and all in them, who have renounced every selfish desire and sense craving tormenting the heart. Neither agitated by grief nor hankering after pleasure, they live free from lust and fear and anger.... Fettered no more by selfish attachments, they are neither elated by good fortune nor depressed by bad."[7] Similarly, in his very first teaching, the Buddha proclaimed that all suffering is caused by craving and that we can put an end to it by working with our minds. To me, this sounds like a way to uncover intrinsic hope!

So now, let's consider the features of intrinsic hope.

First, I'd like to expand on one I have already mentioned. Intrinsic hope is an inner orientation to life that is not emotionally attached to achieving outcomes in the external world. This may sound as if it is indifferent to what's happening in the world—that it is emotionally cold or detached and doesn't care about anyone or anything. But intrinsic hope actually loves the world passionately and intensely. It's just that it is not emotionally caught up in attaining particular results. With intrinsic hope, we accept what is happening—whether we like it or not—*because* we love the world so much. In this way, intrinsic hope is about aspiration rather than expectation, possibility rather than anticipation. With intrinsic hope, I can aspire to help build a peaceful, just, and sustainable world, but I don't expect life to conform to my wishes. I do what I can to stop the global eco-social crisis, but I understand that I may not actually achieve anything. Whatever action we take can be its own reward. We do what we can in the moment, and in the next one after that, and in the one after that, and so on. In this way, intrinsic hope is about taking small steps rather than making big plans.

Letting go of the results of our personal actions can be especially hard because we all want to achieve things in our lives. But as theologian Thomas Merton warned, "Do not depend on the hope of results...you may have to face the fact that your work will be apparently worthless and even achieve no result at all, if not perhaps results opposite to what you expect. As you get used to this idea, you start more and more to concentrate not on the results, but on the value, the rightness, the truth of the work itself."[8] Thich Nhat Hanh makes a similar point about the mundane task of washing the dishes. He says: "There are two ways to wash the dishes. The first is to wash the dishes in order to have clean dishes and the second is to wash the dishes in order to wash the dishes.... If while washing the dishes, we think only of the cup of tea that awaits us, thus hurrying to get the dishes out of the way as if they were a nuisance, then we are not 'washing the dishes to wash the dishes.'"[9] Intrinsic hope washes the dishes just to wash the dishes because that's what needs to be done. It is not thinking about how long it will take to wash the dishes and it is not anticipating the cup of tea afterwards. In the same way, we can work on environmental and social problems and do whatever needs to be done without worrying about achieving anything.

Because intrinsic hope is totally engaged in the present moment, it is open to possibilities and does not have a fixed view of the future. It has aspirations but it does not have expectations about whether, when or how they will be fulfilled. It acknowledges the mess we're in but sees it as an opportunity, not only a problem. With intrinsic hope, we have one foot firmly planted in the present moment and the other reaching out into the uncertain and unknowable landscape of the future. Then we use our ingenuity to build a bridge between them. For example, homelessness is seen as a big problem in Seattle, just as it is in many cities. Well-meaning social service agencies and nonprofits have tried everything, but it continues to get worse. Then in 2015 some local students shook things up when they saw the problem as an opportunity. After connecting the dots between their desire to learn home building skills, the lack of affordable housing, and the latest developments in small-scale housing, they offered to construct some tiny houses, find a suitable location for them, and donate them to those in need.

Although their idea has not eradicated homelessness, these tiny homes now provide safe housing for many in need. Furthermore, the students learned about homelessness, built personal relationships with homeless people, made a valuable contribution to the community, and rallied their schools to support a positive social change, as well as learning the skills they wanted.

Similarly, intrinsic hope means staying positive about the global eco-social crisis. It means saying "YES!" to life and working with the situation. It means accepting what is happening but not seeing it as the only truth. Despite what's happening, and perhaps because of it, we can be creative and innovative. Using the present as a springboard, we can imagine a better world. Indeed, living courageously in these troubled times requires one of the largest leaps of imagination ever taken by our species. Not only must we have the courage to face our fears and anxieties, we must launch ourselves into a very uncertain future with all the faith and conviction we can muster.

Intrinsic hope understands that our state of mind doesn't have to depend on whether our hopes are fulfilled or not. We can choose to be positive whatever happens. This is not about pretending that everything is OK and putting on a smiley face. It is about rolling up our sleeves and getting on with it. As educator David Orr declared "Hope is a verb with its sleeves rolled up."[10] In this way, intrinsic hope is based on the conviction that we have enough and know enough to take action. Unlike extrinsic hope, it doesn't dwell in the land of dissatisfaction, discontent, and inaction; it lives in the land of action, possibility, and potential.

At its core, intrinsic hope arises from a deep love of life. It is a warmth that wells up in our hearts and seeks expression in our actions. It's about doing the right thing because we are loving, kind people and we want our actions to be loving and kind. Most importantly, this type of hope understands that the commonalities between people are greater than the differences. It understands that everyone wants to be happy and healthy, safe and secure. By appreciating these and other shared aspirations, intrinsic hope transcends the divisions between "me" and "you," and between "us" and "them." With intrinsic hope, we stop objectifying other people and see they are just like us so we can love them just as we love ourselves. In the same way, intrinsic hope has a love of the earth. It understands that we are one with her—not separate in any way. We are made from her, sustained by her, and will return to her, so we can love her just as we love ourselves.

The love of intrinsic hope always leads to action. It cannot sit idly by when bad things happen. To illustrate this point, imagine your child is dying from cancer. Do you abandon her because there is no hope of recovery, or do you care for her no matter what? The choice is obvious. In fact, there is no choice. You do whatever you can to alleviate her suffering for as long as she lives. Similarly, we can take action on environmental and social problems, even though it may be too late. Instead of pinning our hopes on achieving specific outcomes, we can ask what is required of us in the moment, and just take the next step—whatever it is. As Frances Moore Lappé said, "Hope is not what we find in evidence, it's what we become in action."[11]

That said, sometimes there isn't much we can do, except bear witness to the world's pain and suffering. We can't stop pollution, climate disruption, or species extinction singlehandedly, but we can always bear witness. Bearing witness can be a very powerful form of action, as demonstrated by Quakers and others who practice this type of nonviolent protest. Thich Nhat Hahn recognized this when he said "The most precious gift we can offer others is our presence."[12] In this way, intrinsic hope is never a passive statement of intent or a bystander exhorting others to do something. It is always a full participant in life.

A final point about intrinsic hope—it can never be exhausted. Because it is inherent in life and motivated by love, it can never be completely used up or depleted. It is a limitless resource. The more we live from intrinsic hope, the more we have. This distinguishes it from extrinsic hope, which we lose as soon as we don't get what we want.

At this point, it might be helpful to summarize and compare the key features of extrinsic and intrinsic hope. So here is a table that does this.

Extrinsic and Intrinsic Hope Compared

EXTRINSIC HOPE	INTRINSIC HOPE
An external orientation to life.	An internal orientation to life.
Expects or anticipates specific outcomes. Emotionally attached to achieving particular results. Believes life should conform to its wishes.	Lets go of specific outcomes and achieving particular results. Has aspirations but is not emotionally attached to achieving them in a specific time frame.
Knows what's best. A fixed view of the future.	Open to possibilities. Humble, curious, and creative.
Based on dissatisfaction with life and a lack of acceptance.	Based on satisfaction and an acceptance of life, just as it is, even if we don't like it.
Always accompanied by fear.	Motivated by love.
Leads to disappointment, self-righteous anger and frustration, shame and guilt, sadness and despair, and grief when life does not conform to our hopes.	N/A
Avoids the present moment and lives in the future, thereby precluding effective action.	Lives in the present moment.
Makes plans and fantasizes.	Takes small steps.
Action not guaranteed.	Action guaranteed.
Disappears when our hopes are not fulfilled.	A limitless resource.

The Relationship Between Intrinsic and Extrinsic Hope

The previous section compared (and contrasted) intrinsic and extrinsic hope; now I'd like to explore how they are related.

When I look at my life, I can see that intrinsic and extrinsic hope are not really separate from each other. In fact, they are intimately connected. This is because my intrinsic hope allows me to hold my extrinsic hopes more lightly. In other words, my intrinsic hope tempers my extrinsic hope. Like everyone, I have strong extrinsic hopes, but when I remember that life rarely gives me what I want, and all the difficult emotions that come up when this happens, I can hold them more lightly and remember my intrinsic hope. And with intrinsic hope, the fear, disappointment, sadness, and so on feel less overwhelming and my situation seems more workable. Of course, I still hope to see an end to the global eco-social crisis, but I accept this may be unrealistic. I still hope for a just, peaceful, and sustainable world, but I accept this is unlikely. With this attitude, I feel much lighter, more positive, and more hopeful.

In this way, intrinsic hope makes it easier to live with the fear that always accompanies extrinsic hopes as well as all the other difficult feelings that come up when those hopes are not fulfilled. Speaking personally, I am still afraid of the future and I still feel disappointment, anger, guilt, sadness, and grief but intrinsic hope offers a way of coping with these strong emotions.

Beyond this, there is a deeper connection between extrinsic and intrinsic hope. Paradoxically, we can uncover intrinsic hope when we are most afraid that our extrinsic hopes will not be fulfilled or when we are most distressed because they have not been fulfilled. Extrinsic hope is a gateway to intrinsic hope. This is because when we have the courage to name and explore our feelings about the global eco-social crisis (see Chapter One), our hearts break open so we can experience love. In other words, our pain and suffering for the world reveal the love that lies underneath them. If you think about it, we would not be fearful, disappointed, sad, and grief-stricken if we did not love other people and the earth so much. We suffer because we love.

Once we realize this, we have the means to uncover the intrinsic hope that is inherent in all life. We can use our pain and suffering to uncover the positivity and love of intrinsic hope. We can acquire an emotional steadiness that is not disappointed by failure or hooked on success. We can ride the roller coaster of feelings that come up when we think about the damage humankind is inflicting on itself, other species, and the earth. I have found this extremely helpful. It's not that the pain and suffering go away, but it becomes possible to work with them. The suffering and the love merge together in a poignant bittersweet feeling that is intrinsic hope.

So now that we have uncovered intrinsic hope, what can we do to sustain and nurture it? In Part Two I'll describe six habits that have helped me to do this.

Habits of Hope

CHAPTER 4

Being Present

> *Be where you are; otherwise you will miss your life.*
> — Attributed to the BUDDHA

THE FIRST HABIT OF HOPE I'd like to discuss is being present. This means paying attention to whatever is going on and not getting sidetracked or distracted—in other words, living where life is actually happening rather than in our heads. To understand the difference between being present and not being present, think of a time when you felt completely alert and aware. What was happening? Where were you? What did you see and hear? Chances are you can probably remember the situation very clearly. Then think of a time when you were completely preoccupied by all the thoughts in your head. Perhaps you were upset or worried, perhaps you were planning or fantasizing. Perhaps you were blaming someone for something they did, or perhaps you were justifying your own actions. Now ask yourself the same questions. What was happening? Where were you? What did you see and hear? It's probably a lot more difficult to recall the precise details of the situation. This is the difference between being present and not being present and it's a big one. Now consider how you felt when you were in the present moment and when you weren't. Chances are you feel much more alive and alert when you were in the present moment.

Being present sounds easy, but it isn't. The endless stream of conversation in our heads keeps us from being in the here and now. It's as if an internal committee is always commenting on our lives. Sometimes it is off in the past, rehashing what happened minutes, days, or years ago, sometimes it is lost in the future, daydreaming about what we could or should do in the coming days or years. And, almost always, it is judging, comparing, evaluating, reasoning, or just plain thinking. Although our bodies are physically in the present moment, our minds are usually wandering somewhere else. The French philosopher Descartes said, "I think, therefore I am," but it may be more accurate to say, "I think, therefore I am not present."

One warm summer evening when my son was about eight years old, we were walking on a path beside the Ottawa River, close to where we lived. Actually, my son was on his bike and I was ambling along about 50 yards behind him. I was completely lost in my own thoughts and not present to him or our surroundings. Suddenly, he turned around, looked at me and said, "Check out those raccoons in the bushes." I roused myself from my reverie and looked where he was pointing, but I had missed them and only saw the branches falling back into place behind the rapidly departing animals. I did not see them because I was not present.

If we are not present, we will not see what's happening and therefore miss out on life. Conversely, whenever we pay attention, life reveals itself to us. Being present slows us down so we can see and hear more. It increases our experience of life and lets us relate to our surroundings in a fresh and unobstructed way. Psychologist James Hillman called this "notitia." "Notitia," he said, "refers to that capacity to form true notions of things from attentive noticing. It is the full acquaintance on which knowledge depends."[1] This "full acquaintance" makes everything feel spacious and timeless. In these magical moments when we are completely engaged with what is happening, we forget our sense of self. "I," "me," and "mine" dissolve into the vastness of the present moment. In the intensity of direct experience, the self dissipates like the morning mist revealing the sacred and the numinous. For me, this experience is indescribably hopeful.

Being present also cultivates intrinsic hope because it gives us more choices about how to act and makes it more likely that our choices will be appropriate in the moment. For instance, if you notice smoke coming out of a building, you can choose to respond or not. Awareness of the situation gives you the option of doing something about it—such as calling 911 or rushing inside to see if anyone needs to be rescued. Not being present and not seeing the smoke removes this choice and any actions that may follow.

Only in the present moment can we choose to take action and how to act. We can think about how we acted in the past and plan how we will act in the future, but only in the present moment can we actually decide to do something. This makes being in the present all the more important.

Mindfulness

Being present is not only about noticing what is happening in the external world; it is also about noticing what is happening in our minds. In fact, you can't have one without the other because we cannot perceive anything without the mind. This is the basis of mindfulness. Mindfulness can be defined as maintaining a moment-by-moment awareness of our sensations, feelings, and thoughts, without getting caught up in them. We just notice our experience and simply let it be, without being attached to it or elaborating on it in any way. In other words, we don't think about what comes up in our minds—we can just be aware of the thought. When you notice a sensation, feeling, or thought, you can let it be and gently return your attention to the present moment. If you feel happy, just notice that you feel happy without having an opinion about it. Similarly, if you feel sad, just feel sad. One of the most helpful mindfulness meditation instructions I ever received was to visualize thoughts as if they were bubbles floating in the air and to touch them gently with an imaginary feather so they burst, returning me to the present moment.

When you practice mindfulness, you tune into what you experience in the present moment. It's that experience, rather than the content of the sensation, feeling, or thought that you focus on. You don't need to get hooked by what is going on in your mind, you can just observe it. For me, mindfulness is like sitting outside on a warm, sunny day watching children playing without feeling the urge to join them. You watch them and smile at them, without getting sucked into their games.

To be more mindful, I find it helpful to think about what's going on in my mind as "storylines"—the stories I tell myself about my experience. Things like: "I'm right and he's wrong because..." "She has upset me so I don't want to be her friend anymore." "He should do more to help." Storylines reveal our beliefs and expectations about life and contain judgments of ourselves and others. We all have storylines and there's nothing inherently wrong with them. Indeed, they are necessary because they help us make meaning of our experience. They only become problematic when we think they represent the truth.

Whenever we believe that our storylines are the truth, the whole truth, and nothing but the truth, we are no longer in the present moment because we are so completely enmeshed in our preferred version of reality. This happens to all of us. It's easy to get emotionally attached to whatever we believe is right or wrong, good or bad, fair or unfair. But no one's storylines can ever represent the whole truth. By their very nature, storylines are subjective and partial because we each perceive life from our own perspective. My version of reality will always be different from yours because we are different people. When we appreciate this fact, we understand that our individual storylines about life are never completely accurate. Because of this, there's no need to be emotionally attached to them. As I say to my students, "Don't believe every-thing you think." There are always other ways of perceiving and interpreting any situation. By helping us to see our storylines, mindfulness enables us to be less attached to our beliefs, expecta-tions, and judgments, so we can be more present.

Being less attached to our storylines also opens up new possi-bilities for action. Consider someone who believes that full-blown ecological catastrophe is inevitable. This storyline may or may not turn out to be correct, but regardless, think about how it affects the person who believes it. Not only would they feel completely hopeless, they would not have a reason to do anything positive or constructive. If they could be less attached to their storyline and allow for the possibility that it may not be too late, there would be some space for hope. The point is that we don't have to accept everything we think or feel as true. A thought can be just a thought, without the emotional baggage of belief or disbelief.

So how can we be more present? In addition to noticing our storylines, we also need to understand the challenges to being fully present, especially distraction and selective attention.

Distraction

Distraction helps us to avoid unpleasant and unwanted feelings about the global eco-social crisis (see Chapter Three), but it also prevents us from being fully present. Distraction's ability to dull pain and suffering explains why we are so addicted to it. We don't want to face the mess we're in and all the uncomfortable feelings it evokes. However, the relief offered by distraction comes with a big price tag—it impedes our capacity to understand what is happening and respond appropriately. When we are distracted, we are less present, less aware of the dangers we face, less willing to grasp their significance, and less able to act appropriately. Author Maggie Jackson put it this way: "The (distracted) way we live is eroding our capacity for deep, sustained, perceptive attention—the building block of intimacy, wisdom, and cultural progress.

Moreover, this disintegration may come at great cost to ourselves and to society.... The erosion of attention is the key to understanding why we are on the cusp of a time of widespread cultural and social losses."[2]

The best way to work with distraction is to notice how it operates in our lives. We can learn to recognize the countless diversions we create or encounter every day, understand how we are habitually hooked by them, and actively choose to be more present. Each of these steps requires self-discipline. We need to remember to watch for the things that pull us out of the here and now, understand how they entrap us, and bring ourselves back into the present moment—again and again and again. For example, I know that I am easily distracted by checking my email, drinking tea, surfing the internet, and watching British murder mysteries on PBS. What are your favorite distractions? How and why do they hook you? It helps to know. Then when you notice you're distracted you can bring yourself back to the present. There's no need to feel guilty or beat yourself up when you notice you are distracted. It happens to everyone. You can just be aware that you have allowed yourself to be taken out of the present moment and gently return to it. With practice, you will gradually become more present. None of this is easy, however. I told myself I would not check my email until after I finished writing this section, but I gave into my craving and got distracted. It's about progress, not perfection.

Selective Attention

Selective attention is about focusing on specific features of a situation to the exclusion of all others. It's about not seeing some things because we are too busy concentrating on others. This is the opposite of distraction, but like distraction, it is very powerful. For example, in the spring, I get totally obsessed by the state of my garden, overlooking the fact that spring comes much earlier now than it used to. The phenomenon of selective attention was convincingly demonstrated several years ago in an experiment called "The Invisible Gorilla."[3] In this experiment, observers were asked to watch a short video of six people passing basketballs to each other and to count how many times the balls were passed. During the video, someone wearing a gorilla suit strolled into the middle of the action, faced the camera, thumped their chest, and then slowly left the field of view. When asked about what they had seen, about half of the observers did not mention the gorilla. They had not seen it at all. As instructed, they had counted the number of passes but the gorilla was invisible to them. When the gorilla was pointed out, they were amazed they had not seen it. This experiment demonstrates that people often see only what they want to see, that they don't see everything that's going on, and that they have no idea they are missing so much.

Sometimes we consciously choose what we give our attention to, such as the number of times the basketballs were passed, but often our choices are unconscious. These unconscious choices are influenced by our beliefs and expectations about life. We focus on what we want to see or expect to see. This is called confirmation bias. And it is extremely common. Here's an example with terrible consequences: Early physiologists believed that animals could not feel pain. This enabled them to do horrifically painful experiments on living creatures, despite their cries, screams, and avoidant behavior. The physiologists' beliefs made them deaf and blind to the animals' suffering. Bringing this forward to today, we might ask ourselves how our beliefs and expectations blind and deafen us. What are we not seeing and hearing? One of the things we may not be paying attention to is the pain and suffering we are inflicting on the earth and each other. In other words, we may not be hearing Thich Nhat Hahn's bells of mindfulness. If we were more present to the earth and to each other, we would see and hear the misery we cause and probably act quite differently.

Now that we've considered the two main challenges to being in the here and now, let's look at how they can be overcome and what helps us to be present.

Meditation

One of the best ways to be in the present moment is to meditate. Meditation drops us into the here and now and can be done by anyone, anywhere, at any time. You don't need to be a monk, a hermit, or even particularly spiritual. You don't need to go to a retreat center or somewhere beautiful. You don't need to sit in silent contemplation for hours on end. And best of all, meditation is free.

Many people think they can't meditate because their minds are so busy, but it's not about trying to get rid of thoughts. It is about changing your relationship with your thoughts. It's about training the mind to be less attached to thoughts and examining the nature of mind itself. Meditation is really very simple, even if it's not always easy. At a minimum, all it involves is taking a few deep breaths, becoming aware of the present moment and acknowledging what is happening in your mind.

Meditation is very beneficial. Not only is it calming and relaxing, it helps us become more aware of our experience and more knowledgeable about the nature of life itself. This is why meditation is part of many religious and spiritual traditions. Moreover, numerous studies have demonstrated that it has many health benefits, including lowering blood pressure, reducing chronic pain, and decreasing the incidence of headaches, insomnia, gastro-intestinal distress, irritable bowel syndrome, asthma and emphysema, and depression and anxiety. Some of these effects can be experienced almost immediately. You don't have to be a long-term meditator or dedicate your life to it. Even a few minutes a day can improve your health and wellbeing, just like you can benefit from a little jogging without being a marathon runner.

Whatever hesitations you may have about meditation, I highly recommend you try it. Here are some basic instructions:

+ Find a quiet place where you will not be disturbed.
+ Relax and sit comfortably with your spine erect. Close your eyes if you wish.

+ Gradually become aware of the process of breathing. Pay attention to wherever you feel the breath most clearly—either at the nostrils, the back of your throat, or in the rising and falling of your abdomen.
+ Allow your attention to rest in the breath. Let your breath breathe itself. Don't try to control it—just notice it and let it come and go naturally.
+ Notice the sensations in your body and the feelings and thoughts in your mind. Sometimes it helps to name them. For instance, if you are thinking about what you will do tomorrow, you could say "planning" to yourself. Then gently return your attention to the breath.
+ Remember that meditation is not about trying to get rid of sensations, feelings, or thoughts. It is about noticing them and not getting caught up in them or making them true.

I have had a daily meditation practice for many years and it has made an enormous difference in my life. It has helped me to be more present and more aware of my beliefs and expectations. It has helped me to stay open, calm, and relaxed. And perhaps most importantly, it has helped me increase my direct experience of life, giving me more choices and making me more hopeful.

Using Our Senses

Another way to be more fully present is to use our senses to the best of our ability. Most of us rely on our sight and hearing and are less aware of our other senses. But neglecting some and taking others for granted limits our ability to perceive the richness and fullness of life. So by remembering to use all of our sensory equipment, we can be more present, experience more of life, and therefore be more hopeful. When I walk on the beach near my home on Puget Sound, I try to pay attention to the smell of the seaweed, the taste of the salty air on my tongue, the feel of the wind in my hair and the sand between my toes, the sound of the gentle slip-slop of the waves on the shore and the cries of the seagulls wheeling overhead. This gives me a much more intense, vivid, and hopeful experience of life.

Being in nature invites us to use our senses. It's as if the natural world calls out to be noticed. And when we do pay attention to it, we can be drawn into the present moment without trying. Noticing birds at the feeder, how trees bend in the wind, how flowers orient themselves to the sun, and even the way an ant scurries over the dirt draws us into the here and now like nothing else. It reminds us of the immensity of the world beyond human thought—a world that has endured for millennia and will continue to do so. By luring us into the present moment, being present to nature naturally evokes the experience of wonder.

Wonder

Wonder nurtures intrinsic hope because it cuts through our storylines and beliefs about life. Transcending thought, it penetrates us to the deepest levels of our humanity and lifts us up to the heavens. It affirms life's preciousness, power, and goodness. To me, there is no doubt that a life filled with wonder is more hopeful than one without.

Wonder is about being in the presence of something truly amazing that transcends the mundane and the everyday. It humbles us, lifts us up, and expands our awareness. Wonder is the positive feeling we get when we perceive something that thrills or delights us to the very core of our being.

One of the most profound experience of wonder I ever had took place when I was an awkward and rebellious 14-year-old. One summer evening, after an argument with my mom, I stormed out of our house in an English village, determined to run away forever. After I had gone about half a mile, I found myself in the local churchyard. I threw myself down on the grass between two headstones and wept. I felt angry at my mom and very sorry for myself. My life was so unfair. But then I looked up. The sky was a darkening indigo, with not a cloud in sight. The evening stars were beginning to sparkle against the vastness of the heavens and a thin crescent moon was rising behind the church spire. Some frogs were singing in a nearby pond. As I became more present to my surroundings, I stopped sobbing. After a few minutes of lying there in silence, everything seemed to shift and a sense of wonder gradually overcame me. My perceptions seemed heightened and my feelings deepened. Time stopped. I felt completely at one with everything and everyone. Words from the poem "Desiderata" came into my mind: "You are a child of the universe no less than the trees and the stars; you have a right to be here. And whether or not it is clear to you, no doubt the universe is unfolding as it should. Therefore be at peace with God, whatever you conceive Him to be."[4]

Many years later, I learned that psychologists call this a peak experience. Characterized by ecstatic and transcendent feelings, these experiences can be life changing. Whatever you want to call it, I know that my experience changed me and left me feeling more humble and accepting of life, as well as more positive.

Small children are often full of wonder. For them, every day reveals astonishing new delights. But by the time they reach adulthood, this way of experiencing the world fades and life becomes dull and routine—a burden to be endured or a series of problems to be solved. Naturalist Rachel Carson commented on this loss in her final book, *The Sense of Wonder*, saying:

A child's world is fresh and new and beautiful, full of wonder and excitement. It is our misfortune that for most of us that clear-eyed vision, that true instinct for what is beautiful and awe-inspiring, is dimmed and even lost before we reach adulthood. If I had influence with the good fairy, who is supposed to preside over the christening of all children, I should ask that her gift to each child in the world be a sense of wonder so indestructible that it would last throughout life, as an unfailing antidote against the boredom and dis-enchantments of later years, the sterile preoccupation with things that are artificial, the alienation from sources of our strength.[5]

As adults, we often fail to notice the beauty of nature. But there is always something that can evoke wonder, even if you live in a downtown high-rise apartment. You can appreciate the way the clouds scud across the day-blue sky or the way the rain feels on your face. You can marvel at the wildflowers in a vacant lot, or the spiders' webs glistening with pearls of early morning dew. You can appreciate the warmth of the sun or the light of the moon.

You don't have to leave home, go on a fancy vacation, or spend a lot of money to experience wonder. By training ourselves to experience life's magnificence wherever we are, we can recover a childlike sense of wonder. I feel great reverence for the trees where I live in the Pacific Northwest. Sometimes I lie down on the mosses and ferns of the forest floor and look up at the Douglas firs, cedars, and hemlocks towering over me, their trunks rising straight out of the earth, their arching branches vaulting high above me. I feel as if I am in a holy place, a cathedral made of life itself. Wherever we live, we can experience wonder and be astonished at the everyday, every day of our lives.

Bearing Witness

Just as wonder nurtures intrinsic hope, so does bearing witness to life. Bearing witness means seeing what is happening and then reporting what we have seen to others. It's like being a witness in court who has seen a crime being committed and then testifies about what they saw to the judge and jury. To be a good witness, you need to observe and describe accurately, with as little inter-pretation, judgment, or emotional attachment as possible. Just the facts, as you saw them.

Bearing witness is a very powerful act because it relies on our experience rather than on what we think or feel about it. It reports what we observed, without embellishment or interpretation. By circumventing our opinions, bearing witness gets to the heart of the matter in a very direct way. It also creates a connection between us and whatever we are bearing witness to. By acknowledging what we have seen, we establish a relationship with it and allow others to have a relationship with it too. In this way, bearing witness affirms our interdependence.

Whether we are bearing witness to the wonder of life or to pain and suffering, it can nurture intrinsic hope. In 1989, I addressed the International Joint Commission (IJC) about the health effects of toxic chemicals in the Great Lakes. At the time, I was the Canadian co-chair of the IJC's Health Committee and heavily pregnant with my son. Without thinking about it in advance, I used the opportunity to bear witness to the ubiquitous presence of toxic chemicals in the environment and in human beings. I looked at the Commissioners and the audience of several hundred people and said: "The child I am carrying is currently receiving the heaviest loadings of toxic chemicals that it will receive in its lifetime." The room fell utterly silent. You could have heard a pin drop. All eyes turned to my bulging belly as the power of my words resonated throughout the auditorium. Although the moment soon passed, I felt I had spoken a truth that needed to be expressed and this made me feel stronger and more hopeful.

Bearing witness can be a form of nonviolent resistance, especially when it is done by a group. Sometimes, nothing needs to be said. People can draw attention to their witness simply by their physical presence. For instance, Quakers are well known for bearing witness to war and violence by standing together in silence in public places and holding up banners proclaiming their message of peace. As a Quaker myself, I believe that bearing witness is part of our responsibility to each other and to the earth.

Being Present to the Universe

I would like to conclude this chapter by considering what it means to be present to this mysterious, vast, and ever-changing universe. So far, I have talked about being present to life in a small-scale way but what if we take a much larger perspective? What if we consider astronomer Carl Sagan's revelation that "we are a way for the cosmos to know itself?"[6] What does this do to nurture intrinsic hope?

This astonishing insight makes sense to me. After all, we are made from the universe. Every single atom in our bodies—the calcium in our bones, the iron in our blood, the carbon in our cells—was created billions of years ago in a star, all except atoms of hydrogen and a few other light elements that were formed even earlier, shortly after the Big Bang about 13.7 billion years ago. And it isn't just our physical bodies. Everything humankind can know, think, feel, imagine, or dream comes from the universe. In other words, consciousness must be a property of the universe itself.

In this way, the existence of our species is a way for the universe to know itself. Through human consciousness, the universe is becoming aware of itself. Without any conscious beings could the universe be aware of itself? Thomas Berry put it this way: "In reality the human activates the most profound dimension of the universe itself, its capacity to reflect on and celebrate itself in conscious self-awareness."[7] To me, this is a truly awe-inspiring source of intrinsic hope.

✳ *TRY THIS*

1. Whenever you remember to do so, ask yourself "Am I present?" or "Where am I right now?" Make these questions a regular practice in your life. Notice what happens when you check in with yourself like this—you naturally find yourself in the present moment.

2. Stop whatever you are doing and quietly observe what is happening around you right now. Bring all your attention to your senses. What do you see? What do you hear? What do you touch, smell, or taste? Don't think about it, just experience the present moment as fully as you can.

3. Remember to pause several times a day and take three deep breaths. Pay attention to the inhale and the exhale and then notice any sensations, feelings, or thoughts. Don't get caught up in them. Just observe them and let them go.

CHAPTER 5

Expressing Gratitude

> *We are all thankful to our Mother, the Earth, for she gives*
> *us all that we need for life. She supports our feet as we walk*
> *about upon her. It gives us joy that she continues to care for us*
> *as she has from the beginning of time. To our Mother,*
> *we send greetings and thanks. Now our minds are one.*
> —— From the Haudenosaunee Thanksgiving Address

EXPRESSING GRATITUDE cultivates intrinsic hope. This practice is deeply embedded in Native American cultures and is exemplified by the Thanksgiving Address of the Haudenosaunee people. In addition to thanking our Mother, the Earth, this Address expresses gratitude to the waters, the animals, the sun, the Creator, and many other beings that help sustain human life.

I have learned a lot about gratitude from Native American cultures. For almost a decade, I was chief scientist on a government-funded project to assess the health effects of environmental contaminants on First Nations communities in the Canadian Great Lakes basin. During that time, I led many scientific studies in these communities, and as a result, I spent a lot of time working with the people who lived there. One of things that impressed me was that they would start every meeting, gathering, or ceremony by offering their thanks and gratitude for the gift of life.

This practice had the effect of reminding everyone about the preciousness of human existence and set an appreciative and positive tone for whatever followed.

Sadly, gratitude seems to be playing a decreasing role in Western culture. Today, few people take time to appreciate the gifts they have received. Even the time-honored traditions of sending thank you cards and offering appreciation to the cook after a good meal seem to be disappearing. A few years ago, the US Thanksgiving holiday was usurped by advertisers who promoted it as the ThanksGetting holiday. Thankfully (pun intended), a strong public backlash seems to have put an end to this.

The diminishing role gratitude plays in Western culture is troubling for many reasons, including the fact that there is a correlation between gratitude and hopefulness. This connection makes sense—the more grateful we feel, the more hope we experience. The authors of one scientific study on "the grateful disposition" reported that "ratings of the grateful disposition were correlated with measures of positive emotionality and well-being, including... hope."[1] Making the same point more poetically, Cuban-American author and journalist Margarita Engle said: "My heart drums with gratitude. My thoughts sing with hope."[2] There is also a relationship between gratitude and health. Whenever we feel grateful, our bodies relax, our shoulders drop, our jaws unclench, and tension seems to melt away. Moreover, feeling grateful has been associated with a stronger immune system, fewer aches and pains, lower blood pressure, better sleep and feeling more refreshed on waking, taking more physical exercise, and taking better care of one's health.[3] In this way, gratitude benefits the person experiencing it as well as the recipient.

When we are grateful, we naturally become more hopeful. By recognizing and appreciating the gifts we have been given, gratitude breeds hope. Gratitude doesn't deny the mess we are in, but it does offer a different way of being with our problems because it understands that life is a gift to be treasured. It says thank you for big things, such as someone saving your life, as well as small ones, such as someone holding a door open for you. We can express gratitude for anything that brings a smile to our faces and cheerfulness to our hearts. It's what gets poured into the glass to make it half full. It's counting our blessings, not only our problems.

Gratitude builds intrinsic hope because it helps us to face bad news. It's not that pain and suffering go away, it's that they get put in a different perspective. When I heard about the massive 2014 landslide in Oso, Washington, which killed 43 people and left many others homeless, I felt heartbroken for all the victims and their families. I only live about 50 miles away and I knew several people who lost their homes. But in the aftermath I also felt profoundly grateful for the way people responded. Everyone wanted to help. Emergency workers toiled around the clock rescuing survivors, and later recovering bodies. Grocery stores donated food and water to feed the hundreds of displaced people. Volunteers and relief organizations cooked meals, contacted relatives, and arranged emergency accommodations. Complete strangers sent money, clothes, blankets, and other supplies. The outpouring of love and generosity was truly incredible. I felt so grateful and appreciative to live in a country where people still open their hearts to complete strangers. This helped me cope with my sadness and helped me feel hopeful.

Gratitude also cultivates intrinsic hope by strengthening our relationships with others. When we express our appreciation to people who have helped us, we reinforce the connections between us. The reciprocal exchange of assistance and gratitude makes us feel more connected and more trusting. But it's not only a question of giving back to those who have given to us. Gratitude can also motivate us to benefit people who have not given us anything. This is because we can feel inspired to help them, just because we have been helped by others. Do you remember the Hollywood movie *Pay It Forward* (2000)? In it, young Trevor McKinney is given an intriguing assignment by his new social studies teacher.

The assignment is to think of something to change the world and then to put it into action. Trevor comes up with the idea of paying good deeds forward. In other words, rather than repaying a good deed to the person who did it, he repaid it with new good deeds for other people. Trevor's efforts to pay it forward transform his life and reach an ever-widening circle of people he does not know. The moral of the story is obvious—appreciating others by paying it forward can make us all happier and more hopeful. By paying it forward, gratitude becomes more than just a closed circle of giving and receiving with those we know; it is extended outward towards people we do not know thereby creating new relationships and connections.

These are just a few of the many benefits of gratitude. But even after we think we've reaped its rewards, gratitude is the gift that keeps on giving. This is because every time we remember our initial gratitude, it recreates itself and we feel grateful all over again.

Choosing to Feel Grateful

It can be difficult to feel grateful when there's so much bad news. But gratitude is like intrinsic hope—it does not depend on our external circumstances or conditions. Rather, it is an attitude of mind, an inside job we can choose to feel every moment of every day. Things do not have to be going well for us to express gratitude, and even on the worst days we can give thanks. This may sound strange, but it's true. Let me give you an example. I have a friend who gets very depressed about the state of the world, so much so that she has decided not to have children. One day, there was a major terrorist attack in the Middle East and hundreds of innocent people were killed or wounded. I happened to be watching the TV news with her that day and she burst into tears with sadness and grief. All she could see was a world of increasing violence, bloodshed, and religious fundamentalism. I held her while she sobbed. After a while, she stopped and thanked me for being there with her. Even though she was feeling hopeless about the future, she was grateful to me. Despite, and perhaps because of her hopelessness, she could appreciate my presence.

So how can we be grateful for the gift of life at the same time as our hearts are breaking about the global eco-social crisis?

The first step is to become aware of everything we have been given. We don't have to forget everything that's wrong, but we do need to recognize all the ways we have been helped and supported in our lives. Just taking a few minutes each day to count the blessings in our lives is a very effective way to cope with negative information and emotions. Writing a gratitude journal for five minutes a day can make people feel happier.[4] Try it and see if it works for you. Here's another option: every time you feel sad or depressed, you can remember something or someone that you appreciate. This is not to negate or avoid painful feelings. On the contrary, remembering to be grateful helps us to bear these emotions without running away from them. The more we can be thankful for our lives, the more we can bear sadness and grief. With this in mind, here are a few things we can be grateful for.

Things To Be Grateful For

We can all be grateful for the gift of life. To be part of this wonderful and mysterious universe is a gift. To live on this beautiful blue-green planet is a gift. To have eyes to see and ears to hear is a gift. To be able to think and feel, laugh and cry is a gift. To be self-aware and have a capacity for self-reflection is a gift. All of these things can inspire gratitude.

We can be grateful for the circumstances of our lives. Chances are, you can afford the basic necessities of life and don't have to worry about having a roof over your head or where your next meal is coming from. Many do not enjoy such blessings. Those of us who don't have to worry about these things can be very appreciative of our good fortune. To remind myself of all the lifestyle gifts I enjoy I sometimes ask myself what it would be like if someone living in abject poverty from the poorest country in the world magically appeared in my life and hung out with me for a day. What would they most appreciate about my life? Using a flush toilet? Taking a shower? Going to the grocery store? Sleeping in a comfortable bed? We have so much to be grateful for, yet we often take these things for granted.

As well as being grateful for all the gifts we have received, we can be grateful for the problems in our lives—because they can be opportunities. As social reformer and author John W. Gardner said, "Life is full of golden opportunities, carefully disguised as irresolvable problems."[5] Life gives us numerous opportunities that we regard as problems. But inside every problem there is an opportunity, if we are willing to see it. All it takes is re-framing the situation and seeing its possibilities, as well as its constraints.

Indeed, we can be very grateful that we live in these troubled times because we have a unique opportunity to re-invent the world's economic, social, and political systems. It's true that we face an unprecedented crisis but it also offers many possibilities. As much as we face huge dangers, this is also a time of great opportunity. The possibilities of this moment in history are enormous. The worse things get, the more creative and innovative human beings will become. We live at a time when humankind is being roused into wakefulness, and this is a gift that we can be grateful for. As British playwright Christopher Fry wrote:

> Thank God our time is now when wrong
> Comes up to face us everywhere,
> Never to leave us till we take
> The longest stride of soul we humans ever took.[6]

We can be grateful for everyone who has gone before us, especially those who have tried to build a just, healthy, and sustainable world. They light a path into the future with their passion and enthusiasm. We are standing on their shoulders. The world would be in a worse situation without their struggles and sacrifices and we would not be who we are today without them. I think of everyone who has dedicated their life to peace and justice. Not only the famous and well-known, like Mohandas Gandhi, Martin Luther King Jr., and Nelson Mandela, but also the millions of men and women whose names I will never know.

I feel especially grateful to my mentors—the men and women who have guided and supported me throughout my adult life. In particular, I think of my boss at the City of Toronto in the 1980s, Dr. Sandy Macpherson, who was the Medical Officer of Health when I set up its Environmental Protection Office. I was only 26 years old when I started work for him and it was my first full-time, professional job. I was idealistic, naïve, and impatient. Sandy took me under his wing and mentored me. After the working day, he would invite me into his office to talk about environmental health or whatever was on his mind, and on Fridays we would go across the street to a local bar for a drink. But it wasn't so much what Sandy said, it was more his attitude to life that taught me so much. He was completely dedicated to his job and to doing whatever he could to improve public health. He was also positive, encouraged me to try new things, and asked a lot of questions. In doing so, he made me think and reach my own conclusions rather then telling me what to do or say. I am deeply grateful to him, and to all my mentors.

We can be thankful for those who will come after us. I think of my son, his wife, and their friends and all of the young people I have been privileged to know and teach over the years. They will pick up the torch when my generation puts it down. They will continue the work of remaking the world in ways that I cannot imagine. As their turn comes, they will take on the responsibility of building a better world.

Perhaps most importantly, we can be grateful for the earth. She sustains and supports us. Without the earth, we could not live. Without the sun, the rain, and the soil, we could not grow any food. Without the oxygen produced by trees, freshwater in rivers, streams and aquifers, and countless other natural resources, we would all perish. Life would be impossible without these things, yet we usually take them for granted and rarely consider their importance in our lives. Indeed, it may be that we will only realize the true value of the planet's life support systems after we have destroyed them. By then it will be too late. So can we start to appreciate and give thanks for the earth and all her bounty before we lose it all?

There is so much to be grateful for. Our lives are filled with countless gifts, if only we can see them. Too often we don't. When we fail to appreciate a gift we dishonor the gift and disrespect the giver. We become selfish and inconsiderate. By recognizing the gifts we have been given, we can appreciate the gift, the giver, and life itself. Freely offered, they are not our birthright. It's not that we deserve them or are entitled to them. Rather, they are the gifts of life and we are rich beyond measure for having received them.

Expressing Gratitude

After we have identified at least some of the gifts we have been given, the second step is to express our thanks and appreciation to whomever or whatever is responsible and to pay it forward to others. Feeling gratitude without expressing it is like walking away from a half-finished job, making a pie but forgetting to bake it, or wrapping a present and not giving it to anyone. We complete the job when we express our gratitude. Whether the object of our gratitude recognizes it or not doesn't really matter because expressing appreciation makes us feel good.

We can express gratitude to everyone who has helped us, including people who love us, people who challenge us, people who serve us, and people we work with. Whether we like them or not should not affect our gratitude because every relationship can be a gift and teach us something. Indeed, people who irritate or annoy us can teach us more than the people we like because we can learn patience and tolerance from them. There are so many ways to express gratitude, including saying thank you, offering a smile, a gesture of appreciation or a compliment, writing a note or sending a card, giving a gift—either a physical gift or the gift of your time and energy to baby sit, clean up after dinner, weed the garden, or clean the house. Whatever you give, it's important to choose it carefully because choosing the most appropriate gift to thank someone is in itself an act of caring and kindness.

Expressing gratitude to the earth may appear to be more difficult. After all, how can we give gifts to the earth when everything comes from her? But what's important is the intention and the heartfelt feeling behind our actions. Indigenous cultures have expressed their gratitude to the earth by honoring her in rituals, prayers, songs, poems, music and art, and by cherishing her in everything they do. Today, we can emulate their behavior. We can also plant trees, reduce, re-use and recycle our garbage, pick up trash whenever we see it, conserve water and energy, buy less stuff, and do many other things to express our gratitude to the earth.

Whatever you do, do it with your whole heart. Be as genuine and authentic as you can. And even if you aren't always feeling grateful, try your best to practice it. It will make you feel good, I guarantee.

Appreciation and Problems

Although there is so much to be grateful for, Western culture tends to emphasize problems and difficulties. It's almost automatic to dwell on what's wrong with the world rather than what's right about it. Whether it's what we face as a society or in our own lives, there is a tendency to turn everything into a problem. One might say that our culture "problematizes" life. For instance, you probably believe that the global eco-social crisis is a major problem—I know I do. Climate disruption is a problem. Pollution is a problem. Resource depletion is a problem. They are all problems and they need to be fixed ASAP.

It is not that these things, and many others, aren't problems. They most definitely are. It's just that we don't have to get stuck in the negativity of problem-based thinking. Instead of, or as well as, identifying what's wrong, we can take an appreciative approach. This flips our thinking upside down. Instead of focusing on what's wrong and trying to fix it we can appreciate everything we have and then build on it. Instead of seeing only the difficulties inherent in our circumstances, we could see the possibilities. By looking at what is working or what is good about our situation, we can be more positive and hopeful. As one of my friends says, "Problem solving lowers the energy in a room; appreciation increases it."

In this way, an appreciative approach takes us out of a mindset of difficulties, obstructions, and barriers and puts us in a place of power, potential, and hope. It says, "We are not helpless victims; our circumstances give us a chance to create a better world." I am not disputing there are many victims in this world, but if we get stuck in thinking of ourselves only as victims, we will end up feeling hopeless and depressed. We can always choose how to interpret our experience. By choosing an appreciative stance we can look at our circumstances positively and take back our personal power.

Appreciative approaches have already been used to deal with many ecological and social issues, especially at the community level. By focusing on local assets, strengths, and capacities, they empower local residents.[7] Several years ago, some people living in my community were concerned about having access to locally grown, organic food. Instead of seeing this as a problem, they saw it as an opportunity. They decided to identify and map all the community's food assets, including the farms, community gardens, farmers' markets and roadside produce stands, as well as the shops and restaurants selling local food. The physical map they produced was very informative, but more importantly the collaborative process of creating it led to the emergence of a vibrant community-based food movement. Because of their work, more people started to grow and sell organic food and access and affordability improved. In this way, appreciative approaches build community and inspire action.

Joy

Gratitude leads to joy and joy leads to hope. In fact, they are insep-arable. Have you ever met a hopeful person who was sad or a joy-ful person who has lost hope? I bet not. The more joyful we are, the more hopeful we become.

If you express gratitude, you cannot help but be joyful. En-glish author G. K. Chesterton understood this when he said that "gratitude produced...the most purely joyful moments that have been known to man."[8] Consciously feeling grateful reminds us of all the blessings we have received and this helps us to feel joyful. There is a Buddhist story, told by Pema Chodron, that illustrates this nicely:

> There is a story of a woman running away from tigers. She runs and runs, and the tigers are getting closer and closer. When she comes to the edge of a cliff, she sees some vines there, so she climbs down and holds on to the vines. Look-ing down, she sees that there are tigers below her as well. She then notices that a mouse is gnawing away at the vine to which she is clinging. She also sees a beautiful little bunch of strawberries close to her, growing out of a clump of grass. She looks up and she looks down. She looks at the mouse. Then she just takes a strawberry, puts it in her mouth, and enjoys it thoroughly.
>
> Tigers above, tigers below. This is actually the predica-ment that we are always in, in terms of our birth and death. Each moment is just what it is. It might be the only moment of our life, it might be the only strawberry we'll ever eat. We could get depressed about it, or we could finally appreciate it and delight in the preciousness of every single moment of our life.[9]

But hope does not depend on finding joy in our personal lives. Rejoicing in the lives of others also nurtures intrinsic hope. We can look beyond ourselves and delight in the success, happiness, good fortune, and good deeds of others. Their joy becomes ours. It's usually easy to rejoice in the lives of those we love—our children, spouses, siblings, and friends. But this is a rather limited form of rejoicing, and with a little practice we can rejoice in the lives of people we do not know as well.

When he was very young, my son used to play tee-ball. Whenever any of the pint-sized players scored a run, everyone else erupted in cheers. Parents, coaches, and even the other kids. It did not matter which team scored. Everyone rejoiced in the runner's accomplishment. His or her achievement became theirs. In the same way, we can take pleasure in others' happiness. We can be thankful that they are happy and that their lives are going well. Rejoicing in the lives of others makes us more hopeful because it displaces thoughts of "I," "me," "mine," and puts our attention on others. It helps us to break free of self-absorption and unlocks warm feelings towards everyone and everything. By celebrating the lives of other people, we are reminded that everyone has something to offer.

Gratitude and Consumerism

In addition to nurturing intrinsic hope, gratitude reduces the consumerism that is destroying the earth. In fact, human consumerism is responsible for using up natural resources equivalent to about 1.6 planets a year.[10] In other words, every year our species uses up 60 percent more natural resources than the environment can provide on a long-term basis. By 2030, even two planets a year will not be enough to satisfy human desires. This trend is clearly unsustainable. So anything that can help to reduce consumerism offers hope for the future.

Gratitude undercuts the core belief consumerism is based on— that human happiness depends on buying things. This belief has been very intentionally fostered by the advertising industry. Indeed, the sole purpose of this industry is to persuade us that purchasing more stuff will automatically lead to a better quality of life and hence more happiness. A new car or cell phone, a treatment for erectile dysfunction, a meal from McDonalds or toilet paper. It really doesn't matter. The advertising industry wants us to believe that we will only be happy if we buy whatever it is selling. Just watch some TV commercials to see if this is true. Their message is always the same: "Buy this product and your life will be better." This strategy was very carefully crafted in the years after World War II, when the US government wanted to grow the domestic economy. According to Victor Lebow, an American economist and retail analyst in the 1950s, "Our enormously productive economy...demands that we make consumption our way of life, that we convert the buying and use of goods into rituals, that we seek our spiritual satisfaction, our ego satisfaction, in consumption.... We need things consumed, burned up, worn out, replaced, and discarded at an ever increasing rate."[11] These words reveal the sole purpose of the advertising industry—to stimulate consumerism and economic growth. It has nothing to do with making people happy.

The truth is that consumerism does not make people happy. If it did, people living in consumer societies would be ecstatic by now. But they aren't. Quite the opposite. People who buy a lot of things are less likely to be happy and more likely to be unhappy, anxious, depressed, suffer from low self-esteem, and have problems with intimacy.[12] Furthermore, countries with low consumption rates are often happier than those with large ones. In fact, the three happiest countries in the world in 2016 (Costa Rica, Mexico, and Colombia, according to the New Economic Foundation's *Happy Planet Index*) all have low rates of consumption. Conversely, the US, which has the third-highest rate of consumption in the world (tied with Canada) ranks 108th in terms of happiness.[13] From this, it is clear that consumerism does not deliver happiness.

It's easy to blame the advertising industry but we, the people, must take some responsibility too. Although we are brainwashed by commercials and advertisements—it has been estimated that the average American sees about 5,000 a day—they hit a nerve. After all, if people were not susceptible to them, the advertising industry would not be a 600-billion-dollar-a-year global industry. Commercials and advertisements hit the nerve of human greed. They keep us focused on what we do not have and blind us from seeing all the gifts we have already received. Originating in a sense of scarcity and insecurity, consumerism and greed keep us wanting more and more. But however many things we acquire, we can never be satisfied. Gratitude counteracts this because it comes from a place of satisfaction and contentment that says, "I am thankful for what I have," and "I have enough." Gratitude recognizes that happiness does not depend on material possessions, but rather an appreciative, positive, and loving attitude to life.

✳ *Try This*

1. Keep an environmental gratitude journal for a month. In it, write about the aspects of the environment that you are grateful for. Write about a different thing each day. You could express appreciation for your home or garden, clean drinking water, fresh air, nutritious food, local flora and fauna, beautiful vistas, or anything else related to the environment. Then go back and read your journal.

2. Eat dinner with your family or friends at least once a week. Turn off the TV and *all* electronic devices. Before you eat, invite each person to say what they are grateful for.

3. Whenever you feel tempted to criticize or blame someone or something, flip your thinking and say something appreciative instead. See the positive instead of the negative.

CHAPTER 6

Loving the World

My work is loving the world.
Here the sunflowers, there the hummingbird —
equal seekers of sweetness.
Here the quickening yeast; there the blue plums.
Here the clam deep in the speckled sand.

Are my boots old? Is my coat torn?
Am I no longer young, and still not half-perfect? Let me
keep my mind on what matters,
which is my work,

which is mostly standing still and learning to be
astonished.
The phoebe, the delphinium.
The sheep in the pasture, and the pasture.
Which is mostly rejoicing, since all ingredients are here,

which is gratitude, to be given a mind and a heart
and these body-clothes,
a mouth with which to give shouts of joy
to the moth and the wren, to the sleepy dug-up clam,
telling them all, over and over, how it is
that we live forever.

— MARY OLIVER, "The Messenger"

IN THIS DELIGHTFUL POEM, Mary Oliver connects loving the world with gratitude. This makes sense because whenever we feel gratitude we increase the chances we will act lovingly towards others and whenever we express it to others we increase the chances they will act lovingly towards us. Not surprisingly, loving the world also nurtures intrinsic hope because when we feel love for others, or experience others' love for us, we feel more hopeful.

The scientific word for loving others is "biophilia," meaning the love of other forms of life. Psychologist Erich Fromm was one of the first to define it, in *The Anatomy of Human Destructiveness*,[1] saying, "Biophilia is the passionate love of life and all that is alive." It turns out that biophilia is hardwired into our brains—it is a basic instinct that human beings and other mammals are born with. We all want to love and be loved. In his book, *Biophilia*,[2] biologist E.O. Wilson asserted that it is a product of natural selection because it helps to ensure survival. Biophilia isn't just about sexual desire and reproduction; it's more about life's desire to ensure its continued existence and wellbeing. Babies are a good example. Whenever there's one around, people tend to look at him or her. They can't help looking because there is an instinctive attraction. Babies' relatively large eyes and delicate features are so appealing that people cannot *not* look at them. Biophilia kicks in and this virtually guarantees that babies will be protected by adults. As well as discussing biophilia's evolutionary advantages, Wilson commented that "our existence depends on this propensity, our spirit is woven from it, hope rises on its currents."[3] In other words, the more we love life, the more hopeful we will become.

Love and Compassion

When I think about what loving the world means to me, I feel a deep aspiration for the happiness, flourishing, and wellbeing of other people, other species, and the earth. This could be called *universal* love. In everyday life, however, my love is often limited to my family and friends. This could be called *particular* love. In this well-known quotation, Albert Einstein drew attention to this distinction, and to the need for universal love:

> A human being is a part of the whole, called by us "Universe," a part limited in time and space. He experiences himself, his thoughts and feelings as something separated from the rest, a kind of optical delusion of his consciousness. This delusion is a kind of prison for us, restricting us to our personal desires and to affection for a few persons nearest to us. Our task must be to free ourselves from this prison by widening our circle of compassion to embrace all living creatures and the whole of nature in its beauty.[4]

Universal love goes beyond our personal likes and dislikes and encompasses everyone and everything, no matter what they have done and whether we know them or not. It is unrestricted and unconditional.

Compassion goes together with love, but is a little different. While love desires the happiness and wellbeing of others, compassion wants to alleviate their discomfort and distress. Meaning "to suffer with," it is a feeling of empathy with others combined with a strong desire to relieve their pain. Compassion is more challenging than love because it means being willing to experience others' suffering as our own and do something about it. Even considering this can be scary, so let's unpack it a bit further:

Compassion recognizes that all living beings, including ourselves, experience suffering and want to be free from it. So when we open ourselves to another's suffering, we naturally feel our own. Feeling compassion means that we must be willing to get to know the places that hurt in our hearts—what makes us afraid, sad, or upset. Then we can enter into that space with others and share their feelings. In this way, compassion is always a relationship between equals. It's not the same as sympathy, because sympathy comes with a sense of difference and superiority that says, "I feel sorry for you and I'm glad I am not in your situation." In contrast, compassion says, "I suffer with you, I feel your pain as my own, and I will do whatever I can to ease it." In this way, compassion is always based on a recognition of sameness and equality.

Just like gratitude, love and compassion are in short supply in today's world. We usually base decisions on our personal wants and needs, rather than those of other people or animals. I know I do. To see if this is true for you, keep a record of how many times in a day you put yourself first and how many times you are altruistic and put others first. You could divide a piece of paper into two columns headed "me" and "others" and make a checkmark in the appropriate column. At the end of the day, tally up the results. There's no need to feel guilty if you find that you usually put your own wants and needs ahead of others'. This practice is not about beating yourself up because you are a selfish person. It is about understanding yourself better and perhaps trying to put others first more often.

I encourage you to pay attention to the small choices you make every day that harm others. For example, most people enjoy eating meat but few consider the pain and suffering endured by all the animals that are killed to satisfy this liking. The cruelty and brutality that takes place in slaughterhouses is so horrendous that several US states have made it illegal to take photos or film the process. Even before the doomed animals arrive at the place of execution, they are deprived of food and water and inhumanely crammed together on trucks. Transportation conditions are so appalling that some die en route. Then at the slaughter house, the treatment gets much worse. Fully conscious chickens are hung alive upside down in shackles, shocked in an electrified water bath, have their throats cut and then bleed to death. Larger animals are stunned with a captive bolt pistol or an electric shock, gassed with carbon dioxide, and then have their throats cut. Many suffer excruciating pain before they die. In 2015 about 9.2 billion animals were subjected to this legalized form of mass murder in the US alone.[5] How can any society that allows the merciless slaughter of billions of animals a year consider itself loving and compassionate, especially when it's so easy to be vegetarian?

Not only is vegetarianism a loving and compassionate choice, it also helps prevent climate disruption and protects the environment:

+ At least 51 percent of the world's greenhouse gas emissions are caused by animals raised for human consumption.[6] Their breathing contributes significant amounts of carbon dioxide to the atmosphere and the methane gas they produce contributes more to the climate crisis than global emissions of carbon dioxide.
+ Animals raised for food consume large amounts of water and produce wastes that pollute rivers, lakes, and oceans. It takes between 13,000[7] and 100,000[8] liters of water to produce just one kilogram (2.2 pounds) of beef. In addition, farmed animals in the US produce about 130 times as much excrement as the country's entire human population.[9]
+ Animals are fed a wide variety of hormones, antibiotics, and other drugs that can enter the food chain and contribute to contamination and the spread of antibiotic-resistant bacteria.
+ The global livestock industry is responsible for the destruction of massive amounts of wildlife habitat and biodiversity loss, as well as soil erosion, desertification, and deforestation.

Putting all this together, it's obvious that eating meat causes enormous ecological harm, as well as untold pain and suffering to the animals involved. In fact, many experts agree that eating less meat is the world's best chance for protecting the environment. If everyone reduced or eliminated their consumption of meat, we could avoid the most serious consequences of climate disruption, conserve precious natural resources, and reduce pollution.

Despite the shortage of love and compassion in the world, it is easy to develop them anywhere and anytime. Let's start with love. I recommend working with complete strangers because this helps to develop universal love. It's not as scary as it sounds because you don't have to say anything or behave in a particular way. Next time you are out and about look at someone you don't know. Don't stare at them or try to be noticed; just be aware of their presence. Now think about what their lives might be like—their hopes and fears, their joys and sorrows, their likes and dislikes. Then feel love for them and send out an aspiration for their happiness and wellbeing. Wish them joy and peace with all your heart. This is a great exercise to do when you are waiting in line at the grocery store checkout, on a bus, sitting in a coffee shop, or whenever you are with other people. Buddhists call it *metta* (loving kindness) meditation and I guarantee it will make you feel more loving and more hopeful.

There is another Buddhist meditation for developing compassion called *tonglen*. You can do tonglen by thinking about someone in physical or emotional pain. At the beginning, think about someone specific, otherwise your compassion will be vague and abstract. Hold them in your heart and try to feel what they are feeling. Breathe in their suffering and realize they are the same as you because you experience suffering too. Then, when you breathe out, send them happiness, peace, or whatever you think would relieve them. Opening to other peoples' suffering can be challenging because it evokes our own. But it is the only way to develop compassion. By leaning into suffering, tonglen reverses our normal tendency to avoid it, and this fosters warm feelings towards others and ourselves. Indeed, the more you are willing to open yourself to pain and suffering—others' and your own—the more you will develop a universal compassion that embraces all living beings and the earth.

Many people believe that feeling compassion for others will add to their own suffering. They say things like, "I can't take on anyone else's pain, I've got enough of my own already," or "I need to deal with my own feelings before I can take on anyone else's." Statements like this reveal a common misunderstanding about compassion—that we will be overwhelmed by others' distress and unable to cope with our own. However, true compassion focuses on the person or being that is suffering, rather than the pain itself. So if you take the other as the primary object of your attention, you will naturally feel compassion and won't be overcome by their suffering or yours.

Community

Like love and compassion, community nurtures intrinsic hope. This is true for any type of community, whether it's based on a shared place, a common purpose or interest, sexual preferences, or something else. If you belong to a community, you will likely feel more hopeful than if you don't. There are many reasons for this including:

+ When we are part of a community we feel liked, accepted, and valued. We feel connected with others in an interdependent network and this gives us a sense of safety and security.
+ Community gives us an identity larger than ourselves. It is about what we have in common with others and it helps us see how we fit into the larger scheme of things.
+ We feel stronger when we are part of a community because it has more power and influence than an individual.
+ Communities offer mutual support. They can support us emotionally and physically in tough times. By empowering and inspiring us to keep going, they foster perseverance (see Chapter Nine).
+ Being part of a community opens our eyes to the pain and suffering of others. When we are with others, we can understand their experiences and see what they need. This takes us out of self-centeredness and makes us more loving and compassionate.
+ Being part of a community enables us to be honest and authentic with others and provides opportunities to work through interpersonal conflicts and practice forgiveness—both of which nurture hope.

◆ Communities provide many opportunities to learn, grow, and change. We can acquire new insights, deepen our knowledge, enhance our self-awareness, and share resources.

There's no doubt that communities can make us feel more hopeful, but they can also drag us down. As I mentioned in Chapter Two, hope is infectious and spreads quickly to others. But so is hopelessness. For instance, if you happen to live in a community with high poverty and unemployment, it can be very difficult to stay positive. However, it's also true that many such communities are stronger and more hopeful than they appear precisely because they have been forced to cope with so much. I have seen this for myself in First Nation communities in Canada. In the 19th and 20th centuries, their land was stolen, their cultures destroyed, and their children taken away to residential schools. And on top of this, they were exposed to high levels of toxic chemicals in the wild fish and game they eat. Not surprisingly, alcoholism and suicide became epidemic. But despite all this, many have survived and remained hopeful.

As part of my work with First Nation communities in the Canadian Great Lakes basin, I was involved in a study that measured levels of toxic chemicals in their blood. My job was to take the results back to the communities and provide counseling to individuals with elevated levels. One day, I was counseling an elderly woman in a remote fly-in community north of Lake Superior who had extremely high levels of PCBs, dioxins, and other toxic chemicals. Through a translator—she did not speak English, only Cree—I told her about her results. After some conversation, it became clear that the reason her levels were so high was that she ate a lot of deer, moose, duck, and fish that had been given to her by the young hunters and fishermen in the community. She could not get out much anymore and was dependent on their generosity and kindness.

I soon found out this was not a one-way relationship. After I left her home, I talked with some of the people who provided her with food and they told me they cared deeply for this woman. She had looked after them when they were children and they wanted to express their gratitude to her. But more than this, providing her with food gave them a purpose in life. With few prospects for employment, supplying elders like her with wild fish and game gave their lives meaning. Through the giving and receiving of food, the bonds of community were strengthened and this provided a sense of hope that helped everyone to live and persevere in the harsh conditions of northern Ontario.

In mainstream society, the bonds of community seem to be weakening. Americans are generally less socially engaged, belong to fewer organizations that meet face-to-face, and know their neighbors less than their parents. We're even bowling alone.[10] So one day, when I was teaching a class on communities, I brainstormed with my students on how to build strong ones. Here is the list we generated:

+ Get out of your house and your car. Walk your neighborhood and greet your neighbors.
+ Be welcoming, open, and generous to strangers.
+ Listen to other people. Understand life from their point of view.
+ Tell stories and invite others to tell theirs.
+ Identify what you have in common. It could be a shared problem or aspiration. It could be values or beliefs. It could be that you have kids or dogs.
+ Accept that people have different points of view. Work through conflicts and appreciate everyone's basic humanity.
+ Don't judge.
+ Show up for other people. Lend a helping hand.
+ Be kind, forgive, and don't hold resentments.
+ Ask open-ended questions.

+ Hang out together. Do things together. Organize community events.
+ Share food, garden tools, skills, information, ideas, problems, and solutions.
+ Keep your word. It builds trust.
+ Party together.

This isn't rocket science. It's about being a kind, thoughtful, and caring human being—someone who recognizes that what unites us is more important than our differences and that we are all part of the human community. And there's no doubt that this type of thinking nurtures intrinsic hope.

Loving Places

Just as belonging to a community nurtures intrinsic hope, so does loving places. To understand this, think about a place that you love—your home, neighborhood, or anywhere that is significant to you. It doesn't need to be a beautiful or unique place. It only needs to be somewhere that feels special to you. Now think about how you came to love this place. Chances are you love it because you have spent time there and gotten to know it well. You are familiar with the people, animals, and plants who live there. You are acquainted with its colors, sounds, and smells. You are accustomed to how it feels—the way the wind blows or the way the shadows fall at different times of the day and year. Being in a place and getting to know it is the only way to love it.

When we love a place, we are more likely to care for it and protect it. And when we care for and protect places, we are doing something hopeful for the future. In his book, *Lifeplace*, Robert Thayer explains the connections by saying, "People who stay in place may come to know that place more deeply. People who know a place may come to care about it more deeply. People who care about a place are more likely to take better care of it. And people who take care of places, one place at a time, are the key to the future of humanity and all living creatures."[11] Quite simply, knowing and loving specific places is a hopeful thing to do.

For these reasons, I suggest that you get familiar with your neighborhood. To start, you might consider how well you know it already. Here is a simple quiz I use with my students[12] I invite you to try it.

1. What direction does your home face?
2. What Indigenous Peoples lived in your neighborhood?
3. When was your neighborhood first developed?
4. What are the most significant events in the history of your neighborhood?
5. Where is your library or community center?
6. Do you know your neighbors?
7. Where does the water you drink come from?
8. Where does your wastewater go? If it goes to a treatment plant, where is it?
9. What watershed do you live in?
10. Where does your garbage go?
11. What type of soil is in your neighborhood?
12. What species of trees thrive in your neighborhood?
13. What are the most common birds in your neighborhood?
14. Name some wildlife species that live in your neighborhood.
15. What are some of the native plants in your neighborhood?

How did you score?

If you could answer ten or more questions, you know your neighborhood very well—give yourself a pat on the back. If you could answer between five and ten questions, you have some knowledge—well done. And if you could answer less than five, you have room for improvement. But don't be disheartened. Very few of my students can answer more than five questions without doing some research.

It's a sad fact that many Americans don't know much about where they live. Too busy moving around, they lack deep acquaintance with any particular place. And even though geographic mobility has declined, less than half the US population have lived in their homes for more than ten years.[13] Given this statistic, it is not surprising that most people are not familiar with the places they live, don't love them and don't take care of them.

It can be difficult to get to love a city but now that more than half the world's population lives in one, it makes sense to try. I find this challenging because most cities look and feel almost identical. It can be especially hard to love an urban neighborhood if it is home to gangs, drugs, violence, or other types of crime. But it is even more important to get to know and love these places, because nothing will get better unless someone cares. Whether it's the wildflowers and grasses that spring up in a vacant lot, the residents' resourcefulness and perseverance, the local history, or something else, it's vital to find something to love and appreciate. It's all in how we look at things. It's so easy to see what's wrong with a place, but can we also see what's positive and good? My husband's office is in a rundown urban neighborhood where drug dealers and gangs roam the streets at night, but he has made friends with the sparrows that perch on his window ledge. He feeds them and talks to them and over time, they have come to know him. Even things as small as this can foster hope.

One of the best ways to get to know and love urban areas is to grow things. If you have a garden, great. But if you don't, try to be creative. Some cities, such as Seattle, allow residents to plant flowers and vegetables in the grassy strips of land between the sidewalk and the street and my friend Sam and his neighbors have taken over the strips in front of their homes. They grow kale, peppers, onions, carrots, and so on—enough to feed themselves and donate the surplus to the local food bank. Even if you can only have lettuce in a window box or tomatoes in a pot, you can get to know what they need to flourish—how much sun and shade, water and dryness, lots of fertilizer or none at all. And eating food that you have grown is a recipe for feeling happier and more hopeful.

If you can't grow food, or don't want to, you can buy and eat local food. Shopping at farmers' markets and CSAs (community-supported agriculture) is a great way to do this. My friend, the author Vicki Robin, calls this "relational eating," which she defines as having a conscious relationship with the food we eat and those who grow it, process it, and eat it with us. Towards the end of her book on this subject she declares, "For me the most profound result of a commitment to (eating) local is leaving a legacy of hope and health and, in my lifetime, enjoying the benefits of belonging to a place and a people—the security and love and mutual aid."[14] To me, this says it all.

Loving the Earth

At a larger scale, loving the earth nurtures intrinsic hope. Although it can feel overwhelming to try to love the whole thing in its entirety, I find the photographs of the earth taken from space very helpful. I remember being awestruck by the first high resolution color images taken by astronauts aboard the Apollo 8 spacecraft in 1968. I was overcome by the beauty of the earth—a small blue-green sphere spinning in the vast black emptiness of space. No one who has seen these images, or the many taken since then, can fail to be moved. Witnessing the real thing, Edgar Mitchell, an astronaut on Apollo 14, commented, "My view of our planet was a glimpse of divinity."[15] Chinese-American astronaut Taylor Wang, who flew on the space shuttle in 1985, said, "A Chinese tale tells of some men sent to harm a young girl who, upon seeing her beauty, become her protectors rather than her violators. That's how I felt seeing the earth for the first time. I could not help but love and cherish her."[16]

The view of the earth from space reveals that this gorgeous planet is one, an indivisible whole without any borders or boundaries. It reminds us that the earth is home to every human being that is alive and has ever lived. All their experiences are, or were, contingent on the earth. No other place. Just here. On this minor planet in a minor solar system on the edge of an arm of the Milky Way. This makes me feel very humble.

Despite the unquestionable fact of human dependence on the earth, Western culture still regards our species as separate from it. Indeed, the word "environment" means "surroundings." There's us—and then there's the environment. We don't understand that we are part of the earth and it is part of us. Instead, there's a cultural belief in human separateness and superiority. As Einstein said in the quotation earlier in this chapter, "He experiences himself, his thoughts and feelings as something separated from the rest, a kind of optical delusion of his consciousness." But the truth is that we are entirely reliant on the planet, or as Thomas Berry succinctly remarked, "The human is derivative. The planet is primary."[16] In fact, there's now plenty of scientific evidence that the earth and all forms of life constitute a single complex system, just as it appears in the photographs from space.

Soon after the first photographs were taken, scientist James Lovelock proposed that the earth created the conditions to support life and has sustained them for billions of years. His Gaia hypothesis suggests that the earth may be a vast, self-regulating organism. It's as if the earth is alive and has some type of self-awareness. Indeed, if we look deeply at nature we can see that it is intelligent and not just a random collection of inanimate matter. A seed knows how to grow into a plant with roots, leaves, flowers, and seeds. A river knows how to carve out the easiest path to the ocean. A polar bear knows how to fish for food. In this way, everything has its own type of awareness. Therefore, it makes sense that the earth itself has a form of consciousness too. If the earth is alive and sustains the conditions to support all living beings, one could say that she loves life—not in a personal or subjective way, but in an impersonal or general way similar to the universal love I discussed earlier in this chapter. Although there's no doubt that nature can be very violent, cruel, and destructive, the earth also exudes an all-encompassing love for life itself. I experienced this very powerfully when I was a child growing up in the English countryside.

My father died quite suddenly when I was eight years old. Within a few months, my mother was diagnosed with terminal cancer and started treatment at a hospital some distance from where we lived. Although my physical needs were met by friends and neighbors, I quickly became anxious, fearful, and depressed. What saved me was the love I received from the earth, and the pony, called Pixie, that my mother bought me. Every day after school and on weekends, I would saddle up Pixie and together we would roam the countryside for hours. Rain, wind, snow, or shine, we were a regular sight to local farmers and hikers. In summer, we would saunter through the fragrant newly mown hay fields, while Pixie tried to grab a snack from the bales that lay scattered every few yards. And in winter, we'd stick to the footpaths and lanes, keeping up a brisk pace to stave off cold or inclement weather. During these extended forays into nature, I felt the love of the earth in every cell of my being. She supported and sustained me, her steady and reliable presence reassuring me when everything else in my life was falling apart. Sitting astride Pixie's back, the earth helped me cope with my father's death and my mother's illness. I will never forget the healing love of the earth I experienced at that time. As a result, I fell in love with her.

Many people don't think about their love for the earth (or about her love for us) but taking time to do this nurtures intrinsic hope. In my experience, the more specific you can be about why you love the earth, the more hopeful you will become. It's like when you say, "I love you" to someone. Just saying the words can give you a warm, fuzzy feeling, but when you say exactly why you love them—the way they smile or laugh, their friendliness towards others, or their values and beliefs—your feelings intensify and deepen. Hence, the more you think about your love for the earth and the reasons for it, the more your intrinsic hope will grow.

Here are some of the reasons we can love the earth. We can love her because she is so very beautiful, whether you are looking close up at the petals of a cherry blossom, at a faraway snow-covered mountain, or at the earth from space. Whatever the scale, the planet's loveliness transcends words. Then there are all the resources she provides. We can love the earth because she offers everything we need to live—food, fresh air, drinking water, and other necessities. What's more, she replenishes these resources over time. Trees continue to produce oxygen for us to breathe and the soil continues to produce food for us to eat. The earth gives her bounty freely, without hesitation or holding back in any way. We are truly blessed by her unceasing abundance and generosity. We can love the earth because she is so tolerant of our species. Human beings have exploited her natural resources, polluted her waters, air and soil, destroyed whole ecosystems, and driven countless species to extinction. But despite this, the earth has not judged or condemned our species, but continues to take care of us and support us as best as she can. The earth has been extremely tolerant and patient with our selfish and misguided ways. Do these reasons make sense to you? What would you add?

Loving Future Generations

So far in this chapter, I have focused on loving the world as it is today. But we can also love future generations. Even though the global eco-social crisis has robbed us of the absolute certainty there will be a long-term human future, we can still love the possibility that there may be future generations. It can be easier to love the future generations who are already alive—our children, grandchildren, and perhaps, if we are lucky, our great grandchildren—than it is to love those we will never know. But this doesn't make sense because when people are born should not make a difference in how much we love them. Just as someone's nationality, ethnic origin, religion, gender, or socioeconomic status should not make a difference, neither should the time of their birth. Assuming there is long-term human future, future generations will be born and die, just like us. They will have bodies, just like us. They will experience happiness, sadness, and all other human emotions, just like us. So if they are the same as us, how could we love them less than anyone alive today or less than we love ourselves?

For time immemorial, love and affection have come down from one generation to the next in an unbroken chain. Long before we were born, we were cherished by previous generations. Now it is our turn to cherish those who may come after us. This can be seen in the Native American practice of considering the impacts of decisions on the seventh generation. Oren Lyons, Faithkeeper of the Onondaga Nation, put it this way: "The Peacemaker taught us about the Seven Generations. He said, when you sit in council for the welfare of the people, you must not think of yourself or of your family, not even of your generation. He said, make your decisions on behalf of the seven generations coming, so that they may enjoy what you have today."[18] Sometimes I wonder what the world would look like if everyone based their decisions on this wise counsel.

Loving the world and future generations may sound naïve or impractical, but it can be very down-to-earth and show up in the most unlikely circumstances, such as international politics. For instance, when asked what led to the successful international negotiations for the 2015 Paris Agreement on climate change, Christina Figueras, executive secretary of the UN Framework Convention on Climate Change, responded, "It's love for the planet, for our home, it's love for each other, it's love for those who we know, and we love very intensely because they're in our sphere. But it's also love for all of those people that we will never know, people who are alive today who we will never meet, people who are going to join us in the future and we will never meet."[19] There is no doubt that this type of love has the power to change human history and inspire intrinsic hope. It also makes it easier to accept what is happening in the world today.

✳ *Try This*

1. Complete these sentences:
   - Some things I love about the place I live are...
   - Some things I love about my community are...
   - Some things I love about the earth are...

2. Invite your neighbors over for a cup of coffee or tea. Organize a pot luck dinner, a block party, a neighborhood clean-up day, or a meet and swap.

3. Support a local nonprofit that's trying to make a positive difference in your neighborhood. Donate your time, money, or both.

CHAPTER 7

Accepting What Is

> *We cannot change anything unless we accept it.*
> — CARL JUNG

ACCEPTING THE REALITY of the global eco-social crisis nurtures intrinsic hope because it gives us the possibility of doing something about it. By saying yes to our situation—even a qualified or reluctant yes—we accept responsibility for working on it. But if we avoid or deny the mess we're in, we don't have this option. With acceptance, we are willing to try to make a difference. Without it, we doom ourselves to failure and hopelessness.

Acceptance is the end of our fight with reality. It means we have acknowledged the crisis, even if it feels overwhelming. It means we have stopped denying or avoiding what we are doing to the earth and each other, even if we don't like it. It means we have stopped telling ourselves how life should be, or how we want it to be, and are ready to work with our problems, just as they are. Acceptance can be challenging but it provides the clarity and determination necessary to take effective action. It is like an alcoholic who has hit bottom and lost everything—family, friends, and job. Only when he accepts he is an alcoholic, can he take the actions necessary for recovery. Until then, he will live in a make-believe world, denying responsibility for his actions and deluding himself that he can cope or that everything is OK.

Acceptance is often confused with resignation. People think that if you accept something you are resigned to it. But these two words have very different meanings. To understand the distinction between them, let's go back to the alcoholic. The alcoholic who has accepted his situation probably doesn't like the fact that he is an alcoholic but his acceptance allows him to work with his condition. In contrast, the alcoholic who has resigned himself to his addiction has admitted defeat. He has decided there is nothing he can do about his condition. This passive attitude is both disempowering and self-defeating.

Fundamentally, acceptance is a realization of an unpleasant truth. It takes an idea that has previously been ignored, rejected, or questioned and says yes. It quite literally means changing your mind about something so you see it differently than before. And because you see it differently, you will naturally think and act differently. In this way, widespread acceptance of the global eco-social crisis would change how humankind thinks and acts.

But what would this look like? Not only would we need to accept the scientific facts, we would need to accept the way we feel about them. Although these two forms of acceptance are inextricably connected with each other, it may help to tease them apart.

Accepting the scientific facts means saying yes to the overwhelming evidence that humankind is wreaking havoc on the earth. This is not easy. So if you struggle to accept the scientific evidence, here are some ways of thinking about it that may help:

+ **The weight of evidence.** When the scientific information on a particular topic is incomplete, ambiguous, or conflicting, scientists look at all of it together and weigh how much supports a particular conclusion and how much supports another one. Factors such as the number of studies, their design, the biases of the researchers, and the consistency of the results are taken into account. In other words, scientists weigh the evidence and accept the conclusions that are supported by the most and best quality evidence.

Using this approach, we can ask whether the weight of the scientific evidence favors the conclusion that we are heading for a human-caused calamity or does it support the view that everything is OK? The answer is obvious: the overwhelming weight of scientific evidence indicates we are heading for disaster. In fact, more than 97 percent of climate scientists agree that global warming is caused by human activities.[1] This doesn't deny that some studies may be wrong, biased, or that we need more information, but it affirms the weight of the scientific evidence.

+ **Standards of proof.** In civil law the standard of proof for a guilty verdict is either "the preponderance of evidence" or "clear and compelling evidence" and in criminal law it is "beyond a reasonable doubt." Using any of these standards, it seems obvious that we need to accept that humankind is guilty of causing the global eco-social crisis. There is a preponderance of evidence, there is clear and compelling evidence and it is beyond a reasonable doubt. It just seems common sense to accept that all the legal standards of proof have been met.

+ **The consequences of being wrong.** Consider the consequences if the scientists are wrong and the global eco-social crisis is not really happening. What if climate disruption is all a big hoax, as claimed by some climate deniers? In this most unlikely circumstance, the only negative consequences are that we would have some unnecessary regulations and policies and that fossil fuel companies and others could have saved some money. But on the positive side, we'd still have all the new industries based on renewable resources, currently employing close to 9 million people worldwide.

Now consider the consequences if climate deniers and skeptics are wrong and there really is a massive human-caused climate crisis unfolding. What are the consequences of not believing the science and taking effective action? In a word, unthinkable. Even if there was a 50 percent chance that the scientific consensus about climate change is wrong, would you really want to take that chance? Here's an analogy—would you get into an airplane if there were a 50 percent chance of it crashing? Of course not. Human beings do not require complete certainty before accepting something as a real and significant danger. So why would the global eco-social crisis be any different? It isn't.

At this point, you may be thinking, "Yes, intellectually I can accept the scientific facts, but I can't accept them emotionally." You are not alone. Emotional acceptance is very difficult. It's just too disturbing and upsetting. For climate deniers and skeptics, it seems less distressing to deny, ignore, or question the scientific consensus than to face their feelings about it. In this way, the lack of emotional acceptance can make it impossible to accept the scientific facts. As we are seeing in President Trump's administration, it can also lead to the creation of "alternative facts," such as his earlier 2012 tweet that global warming is a hoax created by the Chinese to make US manufacturing non-competitive.[2]

It's easy to make fun of climate deniers and skeptics or dismiss them as ignorant, but their unacknowledged pain and suffering may be more intense than that of those who are willing to face their feelings. They may feel so afraid that any sort of acceptance is impossible. In other words, they may have to deny the science as a psychological survival mechanism.

As a scientist, I can accept the overwhelming evidence of harm, but I continue to struggle to accept my feelings about it. By studying my experience, I have found that acceptance has at least three different facets. First, there is the struggle to accept my fear, sadness, despair, and grief about the crisis itself and what could happen. I also struggle to accept my disappointment, self-righteous anger, and frustration that humankind is not doing enough about it. Finally, I struggle to accept my shame and guilt that I am not doing enough in my personal life.

This combination is very powerful and I can only stay open to my feelings for short periods of time. After a while, it all gets too much and they overwhelm me, as I mentioned in Chapter One. So I resort to apathy or denial. But then, when I am least expecting it, my pain about the state of the world rises up in my consciousness and washes over me again. This is a conundrum—I can only stay open to my feelings for a few minutes, but when I repress them they inevitably erupt into awareness sooner or later. The more this happens, the more I realize that I must learn to accept my feelings and that I cannot separate my head from my heart. I am a whole person and my emotions are no less important than my intellect. Whenever I try to avoid or ignore them, I create an unhealthy and unsustainable division in myself. Trying to accept my feelings, as best I can, is the only way forward.

This is made more difficult because Western culture values the head over the heart. Objectivity and reason are regarded as more important than feelings and emotions. As a consequence, there is very little social support for doing the psychological work needed for acceptance. There are few places to go and few people to talk with. And many mental health professionals are likely to blame feelings about the mess we're in on one's upbringing or family circumstances.

To be a bit more concrete, I'd like to tell you a story about my own struggles to accept the scientific facts and my feelings about them. My son Jonathan was born when I was 33 years old, after I had been working professionally on regulations to control toxic chemicals for many years. I knew that virtually all mothers' milk was contaminated with toxic chemicals including DDT, PCBs, and dioxins, so it was almost certain that mine was too. The awareness that I was feeding my infant son these poisons at the most vulnerable stage of his life was almost too painful to bear. One of the most loving things that I could ever do for him had been contaminated and I felt angry, guilty, and very sad.

Trying to accept the fact that I was feeding my innocent child toxic chemicals, and my feelings about it, felt unbearable. What made it worse was that no one in the hospital wanted to talk. The physicians and nurses just encouraged me to continue nursing him and said that everything was fine. So I held my son to my breast and suffered in silence, feeling like a helpless victim. After I left hospital, I realized there was something I could do. I could use my situation to draw attention to the problem. So I began taking Jonathan to meetings with government agencies and corporate officials and nursing him at the same time as I argued for stronger regulations. Although I will never know whether my words and actions had any effect, I do know that the experience helped me to gain some acceptance of my situation and reinforced my commitment to work on reducing human exposures to toxic chemicals.

Now that I have outlined some different types of acceptance and some of the challenges involved, I want to suggest some ways to make it easier.

Opening Up to Painful Emotions

Paradoxically, opening up to painful emotions makes it easier to accept them. Leaning into our grief, sadness, and other similar feelings, without judging them or trying to get rid of them helps us bear them and accept them. In fact, when we let ourselves experience our feelings about the state of the world, a strange thing happens—our hearts break open. When we rage about a clear-cut forest or cry about man's inhumanity to man, our hearts soften and crack, making us gentler and stronger, more accepting and more passionate. As Joanna Macy observes, "The heart that breaks open can contain the whole universe."[3] This requires courage because it's quite uncomfortable, at least initially. Not the courage to tough it out, but the courage to be gentle and vulnerable.

When we open up to painful emotions, something transformative happens deep within us. As Joanna Macy and Chris Johnstone say in their book, *Active Hope*, "It is our consistent experience that as people open to the flow of their emotional experience, including despair, sadness, guilt, fury or fear, they feel a weight being lifted from them. In the journey into the pain, something foundational shifts; a turning occurs."[4] This turning allows us to make friends with previously unacknowledged parts of ourselves and to understand their significance. By leaning into fear, we can experience bravery. By leaning into sadness and despair, we can experience vulnerability and tenderness. By leaning into grief we can experience compassion. And by leaning into anger, we can experience forgiveness. Our tears for the world can cleanse our eyes and help us to see everything more clearly.

This transformation happens because love lies underneath all our fear, sorrow, and other painful emotions. Just think about it. If we did not care for other people, other species, and the earth, we would not experience such heartbreak and distress. In other words, our pain and suffering are a natural consequence of our love and compassion. They are two sides of the same coin. As Kahlil Gibran wrote:

> Your joy is your sorrow unmasked...
> When you are joyous, look deep into your heart and you
> shall find it is only that which has given you sorrow that is
> giving you joy.
> When you are sorrowful, look again in your heart, and you
> shall see that in truth you are weeping for that which has
> been your delight.[5]

We suffer because the object of our love is suffering. As I discussed in Chapter Six, this is the basis of compassion. If we love our children, other people, or the earth, we will experience painful feelings whenever they are hurt or in pain. This may sound like a self-reinforcing downward spiral but it is actually very healing and enlarges our perspective on life. When we let go of our psychological defenses and experience our sorrow for the world, we realize our connectedness with others. We understand that we are all in this together. In other words, a broken heart provides the awareness that we are inextricably connected with everyone and everything that exists. It allows us to realize that we are not separate or alone; we are all part of the gigantic interdependent web of life. We discover that opening up to our pain and suffering, and that of others, brings down the walls between us and draws us into community with each other, other species, and the earth itself.

Broken-heartedness at the state of the world has no end. It is not something that happens once and then is over. Because human beings continue to damage and destroy the earth, broken-heartedness is an ongoing state of being. This may not be an appealing prospect, but it creates the opportunity for continuous emotional and psychological transformation. Every day, we can allow our hearts to soften and break so that instead of being controlled by our pain and suffering, we can be inspired by the love that lies underneath them. And this nurtures intrinsic hope.

Forgiveness

Forgiving ourselves and those we blame for the global eco-social crisis makes acceptance easier. It enables us to let go of judgment, blame, and anger and move forward with a positive mindset; however, it requires conscious work and takes time. True forgiveness is always heartfelt and cannot be forced or faked. It often arises when we make a sincere effort to understand people's motivations and circumstances. Everyone has reasons for their actions and when I understand them, forgiveness becomes easy—even if I disagree.

That said, I struggle with forgiveness. Unlike my easygoing husband, I tend to hold onto judgment, blame, and anger, and unless I deal with them they become long-lived, simmering resentments. To prevent this, I try to remind myself that most people cause harm unintentionally because they don't understand the consequences of their actions. No one intended to cause climate disruption. No one intended to cause pollution. And no one intended to cause species extinction. It's true that some corporations knew they were causing harm and did not stop, and that some even tried to cover up the evidence of harm, but to me, this is somewhat different from a cold-blooded, deliberate intention to inflict harm on the environment and other people. Reminding myself that harm is often unintentional, helps me to forgive.

Even if people knowingly cause harm, we can forgive them. Perhaps they are angry or resentful about something. Perhaps they were raised that way and don't know any other way to behave. Perhaps the harm they cause is the lesser of two evils. Perhaps they are otherwise kind and loving people. The point is that we never know everything about another person. And although individual actions reveal something about an individual's character, they do not represent the entirety.

Another thing that may be helpful is being clear about what forgiveness is and is not.

+ Forgiveness happens when we can recall the harm that was done without judgment, anger, or resentment. It is not about forgetting or suppressing our feelings.
+ It acknowledges the harm that was done and tries to understand why. It is not about denying, excusing, or justifying the perpetrator's actions.
+ It is always a personal choice. It doesn't depend on anyone or anything else, including the perpetrator(s). Everyone has the capacity to forgive.
+ It does not require an admission of guilt or remorse from the perpetrator(s). It does not even require a confession or an apology.
+ It is not the same as reconciliation. Reconciliation requires mutual respect among all the parties concerned and the willingness to work together, as in South Africa's Truth and Reconciliation Commission.

+ It is not the same as justice because justice can involve making
  amends, restitution, compensation, or punishment.

Forgiveness can still be a challenge for me. Am I willing to forgive
corporations, groups, or individuals that harm other people or the
environment? Am I willing to forgive Exxon, Monsanto, the Klu
Klux Klan, ISIS, or the Koch brothers? To me, these are important questions, because I care about other people and the environment. My love and compassion for those being harmed make me
question whether I can forgive those who are mostly responsible
for perpetrating that harm. But I do know that when I can forgive
them, I can move towards acceptance.

Most importantly, though, forgiveness is less about what others
have done and more about freeing ourselves from our own anger,
resentment, and blame. While it can make a difference to those we
forgive, its main benefit is for ourselves. When we forgive others,
we feel more positive and more hopeful. By letting go of past
wrongs, we can move forward with an open and tender heart.

Reframing

Reframing is another tool that helps with acceptance. It doesn't
deny what's happening or our feelings about it, but it recognizes
there may be other ways of seeing things. Reframing understands
there are always multiple storylines about reality (see Chapter
Four) and our own particular version is not the only one. By reframing our personal version, we can broaden our understanding
and move towards acceptance. For example, we can think about
the destruction caused by a tornado as an opportunity to build
community, as well as a disaster. We can think about a drought
as an opportunity to learn to conserve water, as well as a tragedy.
And we can think about climate disruption as an opportunity
to develop renewable energy, as well as a crisis. We can even ask
ourselves, what if the global eco-social crisis is happening *for* us,

as well as *to* us? What if it is a unique opportunity to create a peaceful and sustainable human future? This is a powerful way to reframe our storylines and accept our situation because it takes us out of victimhood and puts us in a place of power and possibility.

Our storylines about the state of the world are just that—storylines. Even the scientific evidence is a form of storyline. And if we believe it is the whole truth, we will not be able to see any other possibilities. But perhaps life is not quite so black and white. We can have storylines, but we do not have to believe they are the be-all-and-end-all truth. We do not have to believe everything we think.

This is not to deny that we are facing an unprecedented crisis, but it is to suggest that there are other ways of seeing the situation. Whenever we can reframe it, we reduce the emotional stickiness of our thoughts and feelings, making acceptance easier.

Let me illustrate this. My friend Susan used to have a lot of trees on her property. An abundance of alders had grown on the land after it had been clear-cut a generation earlier. One day, she had most of them cut down. When I saw what she had done, my blood pressure leapt 20 points and I got very angry. How could my friend do this? How could she cut down perfectly healthy trees? In an instant, my mind transformed her into an unfeeling, cruel monster because my storyline was that all trees are good and she was a bad person for cutting them down. I stormed up to her front door and vented my feelings. When I finally stopped, she gently explained to me that alders prevent the growth of other types of trees. It is often the first tree species to grow on damaged land but it crowds out others, leading to an unhealthy monoculture. By reducing the alders' dominance and later planting Douglas fir, cedars, and hemlock, she hoped to encourage the growth of a more diverse, sustainable, and healthier forest, similar to the old-growth forest that had originally existed on her land. This completely reframed her actions for me and I apologized for my outburst.

Reframing our experience nurtures intrinsic hope. It enlarges our perspective by looking at things differently. Try reframing your beliefs about what's happening in the world by following these simple steps:

+ Stop what you are doing and take a few deep breaths.
+ Become aware of your storyline about the global eco-social crisis. What's the problem? Who is responsible? What should be done?
+ Now ask yourself whether your storyline is completely true. If so, how can you know this for sure?
+ Then explore other ways of thinking about the situation. Can you see it as an opportunity as well as a threat? A blessing as well as a curse?

Reframing enables us to tolerate the fundamental uncertainty of our situation. This is very useful because life is becoming more uncertain with each passing year. We can no longer count on anything staying the same for long—the climate, weather patterns, the availability of food and water. We need to get comfortable with uncertainty in all its forms (see Chapter Two). Reframing can help us to do this and this fosters acceptance and intrinsic hope.

Expressing Feelings

One of the best ways to accept our feelings is to express them. When we stop bottling up our emotions, we get to know them. And when we get to know them, their power over us decreases so we can accept them. There are many ways to express feelings about the state of the world. Here are some that may be useful:

+ **Writing** enables us to understand what is in our hearts. It is a way of knowing what we are feeling at the deepest levels of our humanity. When we describe our feelings in writing, we give them shape and meaning, even though it can be difficult to find the right words. Paradoxically, writing prose or poetry, or keeping a journal, makes our feelings more real and reduces their hold on us.

+ **Art and music.** When it is impossible to put feelings into words, these nonverbal forms of expression can do the job nicely, as any artist or musician knows. Art and music do not need to be shared with others or performed in public. They can be just for ourselves. We don't need to judge them as good or bad, attractive or unattractive. We can use these forms of expression to reveal what is in our hearts. In workshops, sometimes I ask participants to draw a picture of their feelings for the world.

+ **Rituals** have always helped humankind to express powerful feelings and find meaning in life. At their best, rituals connect the inner world of the heart with the outer world of structure and form. They create a union between the sacred and the secular. All types of ritual—personal, group, and public—provide a space to express and validate feelings. In doing so, they leave the participants feeling more accepting and more grounded. Group and public rituals have the added benefits of creating and strengthening relationships and building community.

+ **Sharing with others** is a terrific way to express feelings. When we are with people we know and trust, it's easier to be open and honest about our emotions. Over the years, I have found my women's groups very helpful. By simply being present and listening, they have held and supported me. Without offering false comfort or simplistic advice, they have helped me accept my feelings. Workshops that offer safe, trusting spaces for participants to express their feelings about the state of the world, such as Joanna Macy's *The Work That Re-Connects*,[6] are also very helpful.

+ **Taking action** is perhaps the most powerful way to express feelings. Because this is such an important topic, I have dedicated the next chapter to it.

No chapter on acceptance would be complete without mentioning the Serenity Prayer and the important point it makes:

> God, grant me the serenity to accept the things I cannot change,
> The courage to change the things I can,
> And wisdom to know the difference.[7]

Accepting the things we cannot change is the most challenging aspect of acceptance. And if you think about, there's a lot we can't change about life because we are not in control. Ultimately, we can't change how others think and feel and we can't stop the global eco-social crisis singlehandedly. Indeed, we can't really change anything in the external world on our own. The only thing we can change is ourselves, and even this can be difficult and take time. So if we focus on things we cannot change, we waste precious time, energy, and resources. The best option is to accept them and focus on what we can change—ourselves. For instance, I need to accept that I cannot stop glaciers melting, but I can reduce my carbon emissions, work to persuade corporations to reduce their emissions, and lobby politicians for stronger regulations. Similarly, I need to accept that I cannot end homelessness or poverty, but I can offer my time, energy, and resources to those in need, as well as advocate for compassionate government policies and programs. Accepting that the only thing we can truly change is ourselves is very liberating because it frees us up from the futile task of trying to change the world singlehandedly. And taking responsibility for changing ourselves is very empowering because it makes us take action.

Although we cannot change others, we can influence them because we can create the conditions for change. Indeed, when we take responsibility for changing ourselves, we naturally create the conditions for others to do the same. This is huge. By doing our best to reduce our ecological footprints and build a just, peaceful, and sustainable world, we inspire others to do the same. When we accept our situation—however difficult and painful—we can take responsibility for changing our own beliefs, feelings, and behavior and make it more likely that others will change. Whether we are making changes in our personal lives or trying to change the organizations we work in, our churches, schools, communities, or society-at-large, we can all contribute to social and environmental change that ripples out far beyond us as individuals. This is a source of intrinsic hope.

✳ *Try This*

1. Sit in a quiet, peaceful place, preferably in nature. Become aware of your breath. Then lean into your feelings about the state of the world for as long as you can. Observe them without getting caught up in them. Then ask yourself why you have these feelings. Open yourself to the love that lies underneath them.

2. Work on forgiveness. Forgive yourself for your own lifestyle and for not doing enough. Forgive others who have harmed the earth or other people. Try to understand them and offer them your forgiveness.

3. Reframe your storyline. Whenever you think that the world is a dangerous or ugly place remember something kind that someone did for you or something that is beautiful. Whenever you feel anger, sadness, or grief about the state of the world think about all the good people, including you, who are trying to make it better.

CHAPTER 8

Taking Action

> *Hope is an ax you break down doors with in an emergency…*
> *it will take everything you have to steer the future away*
> *from endless war, from the annihilation of the earth's treasures*
> *and the grinding down of the poor and marginal.*
> *Hope means another world might be possible, not promised,*
> *not guaranteed. Hope calls for action; action is impossible*
> *without hope…To hope is to give yourself to the future,*
> *and that commitment to the future makes the present*
> *inhabitable. Anything could happen, and whether we act*
> *or not has everything to do with it.*
>
> —— REBECCA SOLNIT, *Hope in the Dark*

IF WE CAN ACCEPT that the global eco-social crisis is human caused, we have the possibility of taking effective action. Taking action is one of the best ways to nurture intrinsic hope. Transforming an insubstantial thought into something tangible, it breaks us out of apathy and denial. It liberates us from the vicious cycle of not wanting to do anything because we feel hopeless and then feeling hopeless because we are not doing anything. Even if we think there is nothing we can do, there is always something. Just listening to the sparrows chirping outside your window, smelling a fragrant flower, or going for a walk can make you feel more hopeful.

Of course, listening to birds, smelling flowers, and going for walks will not solve all our problems. We need to take much more action than that. So what makes people do something about the state of the world? What makes us get up out of our armchairs and transforms well-meaning intentions into actual deeds? Mostly, we take action when there are good reasons to do so. With this in mind, here are some.

Scientific Information

One reason to take action is that there is abundant scientific information that humankind is destroying the earth and threatening its own survival. What better reason could there be? With all the information that's available, taking action to avert the global eco-social crisis is the logical and rational thing to do. So it's not surprising that many people believe that more research studies and better ways of communicating the results are all that's needed to motivate social and personal change.

I used to be one of these people. As a trained biochemist, I believed that ever-increasing scientific information would guarantee the changes we need. But over the years, many experiences have taught me otherwise. One of them was a study I did in the 1980s. It was on toxic contaminants in food and it was the first nonoccupational, multichemical exposure assessment conducted in Canada. My research showed that, on average, residents of Toronto and southern Ontario received about 85 percent of their exposure to toxic chemicals from food. Air and water, which had been assumed to be the most important exposure pathways, were actually much less significant.[1,2,3] I released the study results at the 1986 World Conference on Large Lakes on Mackinac Island in Lake Michigan and they attracted international media attention as well as demands for immediate government action. But despite my findings, and subsequent studies that confirmed what

I had found, the Canadian government did nothing. This was an important lesson for me.

The sad truth is that scientific information alone is not enough to motivate social and personal action. It plays an important role but it is not sufficient on its own. If it were, humankind would have taken action on many of its problems decades ago. Indeed, we have more information about the harm we are inflicting on the earth and on each other than ever before, but this has not stopped us from continuing to do it. Take climate disruption. There is a very strong scientific consensus that it is real, that it is caused by human actions, and that it is the most serious ecological threat facing humankind today. But despite all the government promises that have been made, including the 2015 Paris Agreement, humankind has not yet taken action on a scale commensurate with the size and severity of the problem.

The belief that scientific information automatically leads to action is based on the assumption that human beings are rational creatures and make logical choices. But the truth is that most human decisions are based on feelings, gut hunches, and deeply-held beliefs. If human beings were governed by reason and logic, would anyone fall in love? Would anyone rush into a burning building to rescue someone else? Would anyone donate bone marrow or a kidney? Probably not. We like to think we are rational and logical beings, but in reality other factors play an important role in our decisions. So even though it is important to understand what science is telling us, perhaps it's time to get honest and admit that we have hearts as well as heads.

However, many scientists and activists continue to believe that more information and better communication strategies are all that's needed to motivate personal and collective change. They fail to realize that the endless litany of bad news does nothing to inspire positive action and often increases people's resistance to change. This is because it's easy to get fearful and overwhelmed by too much disturbing information and then to retreat into avoidant and self-protective habits, such as apathy and denial. And although fear can motivate action, it is a negative motivator that dampens enthusiasm and excitement. For these reasons, relying exclusively on scientific information to spur action to protect the earth is likely to fail.

So if scientific information on its own is not a sufficient reason, what is?

Results, Responsibility, and Virtue

To respond to this question, let's consider what motivates human action in general. At a very basic level, there are only three factors. The first is that we want to achieve particular results. Philosophers call this consequentialism. Does it sound familiar? It should because consequentialism is the most common reason for taking action in Western culture. Consider what motivates your behavior. I bet it is mostly because of the consequences or results you want to achieve. You want to improve things—to make them better either for yourself or for others. You do the laundry because you want clean clothes. You give your wife a Valentine's Day card because you want to see her smile. You save money because you want to enjoy your retirement. Almost everything we do is motivated by the results we want to achieve. Or it's about taking action to avoid specific results that are harmful to yourself or others. You stop at a red light because you don't want to cause an accident. You don't smoke because you don't want to get lung cancer. You don't say something mean to your best friend because you don't want to upset them. Either way—seeking specific outcomes or trying to avoid them—consequentialism always focuses on the results of action.

Consequentialism is also one of the hallmarks of extrinsic hope. As I discussed in Chapter Three, whenever we have extrinsic hope, we are invested in attaining specific results. And even though we don't, or can't, always take action to achieve these results, we still hope that they will come to pass. Just like extrinsic hope, consequentialism is always accompanied by the fear of not getting the results we want, as well as anger, disappointment, grief, and sadness if we don't. And because we don't know for sure that we will succeed in solving our problems, consequentialism, just like extrinsic hope, is a setup for these painful feelings.

Second, action can be motivated by a sense of responsibility. We can do something simply because it is the right thing to do, regardless of whether we actually achieve anything. This motivation for taking action is different from consequentialism because it focuses on the quality or characteristics of the action itself, rather than its consequences. For example, you may feel motivated to pick up a piece of trash on the sidewalk because it is the right thing to do, rather than because you believe your action will put an end to littering. Philosophers call this motivation responsibility- or duty-based ethics.

Responsibility-based ethics are based on the understanding that relationships always come with responsibilities. When you love or feel affection for someone, you naturally feel responsible for them. Similarly, if you love the earth, you probably feel an obligation to protect her. It's just what you are called to do, whether or not you achieve any particular results. Even if you're in relationship with someone you don't necessarily like, you may still feel a responsibility towards them. For instance, you may not like your boss or your in-laws, but you still want to do the right thing when you interact with them. Like intrinsic hope, responsibility-based ethics are based on the belief that we are all connected. You take action because it is the loving and caring thing to do in the circumstances.

Not only are consequentialism and responsibility-based ethics associated with the two different types of hope, they often conflict with each other. This is evident in the basic question about ends and means: "Does a desired result justify any means of achieving it?" For example, if you could save the world by killing someone, would you do it? Or, if a man cannot afford to buy a life-saving drug to treat his sick wife should he steal it? Or, is it OK for "eco-terrorists" to burn down new ski areas to draw attention to the loss of wildlife habitat? What do you think? Consequentialism would say yes, the ends always justify the means. But responsibility-based ethics would say no, the results or ends don't justify the means; the action itself must be ethical.

Although debates about ends and means are fascinating, they ignore the third and least common reason to take action—that our actions should reveal our highest ideals and principles. Often called virtue ethics, this motivation is about revealing human goodness in everything we do. Like responsibility-based ethics, virtue ethics are based on a sense of relationship and connection and go together with intrinsic hope. Virtue is an old-fashioned concept, but it is just as relevant now as it was when the ancient Greeks first developed it well over two thousand years ago. They identified four virtues: wisdom, courage, moderation, and justice. Later, the Catholic Church added another three: faith, hope, and love. These seven virtues can be thought of as the foundation of an ethical life. If we base our actions on them, we will be good, trustworthy people.

Fundamentally, virtue ethics are about moral integrity—about making our actions in the world consistent with our values. Quaker author Parker Palmer calls this living "an undivided life."[4] Living an undivided life is about bridging the gap between our beliefs and how we actually live. It's about being a whole person and walking our talk. When our actions are consistent with our beliefs, we feel better about ourselves and more hopeful. In my experience, when I am true to my ideals, I feel a gentle strength and a quiet contentment. Conversely, whenever my actions are inconsistent with my principles, I feel morally conflicted and distressed.

The most acute moral conflict I have experienced took place while I was working as an environmental policy consultant for the Canadian federal government. After about ten years, I realized

I needed to change careers because the work I was paid to do was inconsistent with my belief in telling the truth. The last straw came in early 2002 when I was asked to write a progress report on the implementation of an international environmental agreement. To write the report, I interviewed officials from the signatory countries, asking them about the policies and programs their governments had put in place to honor their commitments. It soon became clear that most countries had done very little or nothing at all. However, I was expected to dress up this lack of action so it appeared as if the governments had done more than they had. Although I was not asked to lie outright, I was encouraged to embellish the truth. This seemed wrong to me. I wrote the report and did my best to be truthful, but I felt very uncomfortable because I was compromising my integrity. I was living a divided life. Soon after, I realized that I could not continue to work as a consultant in this way. The internal conflict was too great to bear, even though it meant giving up large consulting fees and taking a lower-paying job teaching at Antioch University Seattle. A six-figure income could not compensate for the loss of my moral integrity.

In real life, people's motivations for taking action are usually a mixture of consequentialism, responsibility-based ethics, and virtue ethics, with consequentialism being the most common, responsibility-based ethics being the second most common, and virtue ethics being the least common. Reflecting on my own motivations for taking action, there's no doubt that I want to stop climate disruption, poverty, pollution, biodiversity loss, etc. (consequentialism), but I am also motivated by my love and caring for other living beings (responsibility-based ethics) and by my ideals and principles (virtue ethics). Over time, I have found that the more I think about my responsibility to others and my internal moral compass, the less I am emotionally attached to achieving particular results and the more hopeful I become.

Purpose and Commitment

Taking action on the mess we're in is easier when we have a clear purpose and a strong commitment to follow through. But not just any purpose will do. We need a deep, altruistic purpose that goes beyond our individual desires and centers on the common good, however we define it. Having a deep, altruistic purpose takes us out of ourselves and connects us with our highest ideals and principles (virtue ethics). This puts our lives in a larger context and gives us a reason to live and something to hold on to in the face of adversity. A deep altruistic purpose inspires to help and serve others.

Having a purpose is not the same thing as wanting to achieve a particular result because it is much more open. When we want to achieve a particular result, there is a sticky emotional attachment to whatever "I" or "we" want. It comes with a storyline that says, "I know what's best," and it closes down possibilities and options. In contrast, a purpose opens us up. It is about having a spacious vision for the future that isn't caught up in details or particulars. It's having a direction, but not knowing how we will get there, what the destination looks like, or even if there is one.

Having a deep, altruistic purpose goes hand in hand with commitment. On its own, a deep altruistic purpose is a statement of intent but it only becomes real when we make a commitment to honor it. Purpose gives us something to aim for and commitment does the work. We can have the purpose of working on environmental or social problems, but it is commitment that helps us keep going when enthusiasm and energy falter. Commitment guides our choices and shapes our actions. It can also lead to unanticipated benefits, as described in the well-known quote attributed to Goethe:

> Until one is committed, there is hesitancy, the chance to draw back. Concerning all acts of initiative (and creation), there is one elementary truth that ignorance of which kills

countless ideas and splendid plans: that the moment one definitely commits oneself, then Providence moves too. All sorts of things occur to help one that would never otherwise have occurred. A whole stream of events issues from the decision, raising in one's favor all manner of unforeseen incidents and meetings and material assistance, which no man could have dreamed would have come his way. Whatever you can do, or dream you can do, begin it. Boldness has genius, power, and magic in it. Begin it now.

Making a commitment nurtures intrinsic hope because it gives us the steadfastness we need. Even if we make our best effort to keep our word and fail, at least we have tried. And if we fail, we can always renew our promise and try to do better. Regardless of whether we succeed or not, when we apply commitment to our purpose we become more hopeful. On the other hand, having a purpose without committing to it can leave us feeling depressed and hopeless because we have not even tried.

All commitments are future oriented, so it is important not to enter into them lightly. We need to understand what we are promising to do or not do and we need to be willing to try to honor that. That's what makes commitments so powerful. For instance, a commitment to take the bus to work is more powerful than just taking the bus to work because if you are tempted to drive your car you can always fall back on your commitment. Commitment offers the self-discipline needed to control our behavior. In this way, living a life of commitment is at the heart of freeing ourselves from giving into harmful habits, impulses, and cravings.

Honoring a commitment is much more difficult than making it because we must work with ourselves to notice when we are violating it and take corrective action. Keeping one's word requires sustained attention and effort. Anyone in a happy long-term marriage knows this. You have to work at it, even when you don't feel like it. You make the extra effort because you have made a commitment and you want to keep it to the best of your ability. For this reason, commitments made on the spur of the moment or hastily can be very difficult to sustain. On the other hand, commitments that emerge over time are more likely to stick.

I don't remember when I became aware of my commitment to work on environmental problems. It is as if I always had one. Perhaps I was born with it, perhaps it was a result of my upbringing, or perhaps it came from somewhere else. It is not something I consciously chose; rather, it is something I gradually became aware of. So a commitment is not necessarily something we decide at a specific moment, more often it is something that rises up in our consciousness over time and speaks to us. As Parker Palmer says, "Before you tell your life what you intend to do with it, listen for what it intends to do with you. Before you tell your life what truths and values you have decided to live up to, let your life tell you what truths you embody, what values you represent."[5] I find this a very helpful way to think about commitment.

When we have a deep, altruistic purpose and a commitment to follow through on it, we cannot not take action. This double negative was explored by Larry Parks Daloz and his colleagues in their book, *Common Fire: Leading Lives of Commitment in a Complex World*. Towards the end, the authors comment, "The people we interviewed have learned that they and all others are an integral part of the fundamental interdependence of life. Knowing this, when faced with a violation of what they know to be true, they can*not not* act. Their commitment derives from knowing that we are bound to one another and to the planet; it is as untenable to turn away from the world's pain and unrealized potential as to abandon one's child or sever one's hand."[6] (Italics in original.)

Do No Harm

One commitment we can make is to promise to do no harm to the environment and other people. This is an important first step towards working on the global eco-social crisis. If you are feeling bold, you could also take the next step and commit yourself to benefiting the environment and other people.

But let's start with doing no harm. There are several reasons to make a commitment to do no harm. First, you probably do not want to hurt other people or living beings and believe that it is unethical to do so. Second, if you believe we are all connected in the web of life, it is only logical to assume that if you harm anyone or anything, you are indirectly harming yourself. And third, if you are a religious or spiritual person, you may believe that all human beings, and perhaps other species, contain a spark of divine energy, so to harm another is to diminish the sanctity of life itself.

But even with the best of intentions, hurting or even killing other living beings may be unavoidable. Here is a true story about this. Last summer, my husband and I had a bat in our bedroom. It was a hot summer's night so we had left the windows wide open. Our windows don't have screens so when we leave them open, we are often visited by moths, flies, and mosquitoes. But we'd never had a bat before. That night, one was swooping above our bed in the dark, obviously distressed and desperately trying to echolocate its way back outside. My husband woke up first and realized the identity of our guest. He leapt out of bed and deftly threw a towel from the nearby bathroom over the terrified animal in mid-flight. After it fell to the floor, he quickly gathered the jumble of bat and towel in his arms, ran downstairs, and deposited the stunned creature on the patio. In the morning, we ventured outside to see if it had recovered, but to our consternation it lay dead exactly where he had left it.

Although he wanted to save the bat, my husband killed it. Indeed, human beings and other species cannot avoid doing some harm. Simply by living, our actions can hurt someone or something. At the very least, we trample plants, insects, and microorganisms whenever we walk on the ground. Even if you are a vegan, your diet still requires killing plants. And what about weeding the garden, swatting a bug, or picking a bouquet of flowers?

So how can we commit to do no harm, let alone commit to benefiting others? It seems so unrealistic when we only think about the consequences of our actions. If we base a commitment to do no harm on consequentialist thinking and judge ourselves solely on the basis of the results of our actions, we will inevitably violate our vow. But if we base a commitment to do no harm on the quality of the action itself (responsibility-based ethics) and/or on our ideals (virtue ethics), it becomes a lot more workable. This doesn't mean that we can ignore the consequences of our actions but it does mean that it's important to consider all three motivations for taking action when we make a commitment to do no harm. Furthermore, most of the damage we cause is inadvertent or accidental, like my husband killing the bat. Most people want to be decent and honorable. What's important is making the commitment to do no harm and then doing our best to keep it. We may not succeed, but we can always keep trying.

Small Steps

Even if a commitment to do no harm is not based on consequentialism alone, honoring it can still feel overwhelming and impractical. To make it more manageable, we can take small steps in the right direction. Indeed, this is the only way of moving forwards. As the Chinese philosopher Lao Tzu famously said, "A journey of a thousand miles begins with a single step." So what small steps can we take?

Many people seem reluctant to take even one small step because they think that individual action will not make any difference. They believe that the global eco-social crisis is so vast and complicated that personal actions are a waste of time and energy and that social change is all that matters. Derrick Jensen made this point several years ago in an essay called "Forget Shorter Showers."[7] Although it is true that social change is necessary, this doesn't mean that individual actions are irrelevant or unnecessary, especially if we think in terms of responsibility-based or virtue ethics. If we base our actions on these motivations, shorter showers and other small personal actions make perfect sense.

But there's another reason why small steps make sense. It's because we can never know the results of our actions. Individual actions may—just may—be effective. If enough people take steps to change their lifestyles, the cumulative effects could become significant. As Malcolm Gladwell demonstrated in his book on the topic, there is a tipping point[8] when the number of people who think or act in a certain way becomes a critical mass and social change happens spontaneously. It's the transformative moment when an idea, trend, or social behavior crosses a threshold and spreads like wildfire. Just as a few individuals can start a fashion trend, post fake news that goes viral online, or launch a social movement, so our individual actions could make all the difference. As Margaret Meade said, "Never doubt that a small group of thoughtful, committed citizens can change the world. Indeed, it is the only thing that ever has."

So perhaps it's best to give up on trying to save the world and just take whatever small steps we can. Towards the end of his life philosopher William James made this point when he said "I am done with great things and big things, great institutions and big success, and I am for those tiny invisible molecular moral forces that work from individual to individual, creeping through the crannies of the world like so many rootlets, or like the capillary oozing of water, yet which, if you give them time, will rend the hardest monuments of man's pride."[9]

It's helpful to remember that the entire crisis was created by small acts, many of which caused harm unintentionally. Therefore, it's possible that it can be undone by many small, intentional acts of human decency and kindness. And if we persevere in taking small steps day after day and year after year, we may be able to resolve our problems more quickly than they were created. The point is that by focusing on what we can each do, even if it is something very, very small, we take our attention away from everything we can't do and put it on what we can. This makes us feel more hopeful.

There are plenty of small steps we can take. We can reduce our ecological footprints by decreasing the amount of water and energy we use and the amount of garbage we produce. We can ask ourselves if we really need a new TV, another pair of shoes, or the latest electronic device. And when we do need to buy something, we can buy environmentally-friendly, reconditioned or second-hand products whenever we can. There's no doubt that we, the people, could wield a lot more power over the marketplace than we currently do. Just look at how increasing demand for local, organic food is changing the food industry. By paying attention to the small choices we make every day, we could cumulatively make a big difference.

If you would like some suggestions about small steps you could take, here are a few sources of information:

+ *17 Ridiculously Easy Things You Can Do To Help Save the Earth Every Day.* huffingtonpost.com/2014/04/22/easy-ways-to -save-earth_n_5168684.html. Simple, easy and straightforward article.
+ *50 Ways You Can Help Save the Earth.* ecowatch.com/50-ways -you-can-help-save-the-earth-1882107724.html. Great practical ideas.
+ *How to Reduce Your Carbon Footprint: 365 Simple Ways to Save Energy, Resources and Money,* by Joanna Yarrow. Chronicle Books, 2008.

One small step I have taken is to commit to being vegetarian. I haven't eaten much meat in my adult life, and none at all for the past seven years. This is because I want to reduce the pain and suffering of animals raised for consumption, reduce emissions of greenhouse gas emissions and other pollutants, and decrease use of precious natural resources (see Chapter Six). Indeed, adopting a vegetarian diet or, better yet, a vegan one is perhaps the single most important small step that anyone can take to benefit the environment. And even if you are not ready to stop eating meat entirely, going without it for just one day a week is a step in the right direction.

I want to conclude this chapter with a few words about doing too much. Although taking action is an excellent way to nurture intrinsic hope, it is easy to get compulsive and stay busy all the time. This is very tempting because it makes us feel as if we are being helpful. However, doing too much can itself be a form of denial because it enables us to avoid dealing with our feelings about the state of the world. Environmental and social activists, as well as those working in the helping professions, are especially prone to this. Often working long hours, they sweep their feelings under the rug and pretend they don't exist. It's easy to understand why—they feel their work is so urgent and important there's no time to slow down or take a break. But working all the time is a setup for exhaustion and burn out. And this doesn't help anyone or anything.

To cultivate intrinsic hope, we need to live a balanced life. If we stay busy all the time, we won't have time to process our feelings about the state of the world. On the other hand, if we don't do anything except work on our feelings, we are likely to get stuck and mired down in them. So it's important to find a balance between working with our feelings and taking action—not a static balance, but a dynamic one that changes depending on our current circumstances and frame of mind. I have had days, weeks, and months when I have felt drawn to actively engaging with environmental problems; similarly, I have had days, weeks, and months when I have been more introspective. Without finding a balance between action and reflection it is unlikely that we'll have much perseverance. And, as I discuss in Chapter Nine, resolving the global eco-social crisis is long-term work that will require enormous perseverance.

✳ *Try This*

1. Whenever you feel hopeless about the state of the world, do something positive. Call a friend, hug someone you care about, smile at a complete stranger, visit your parents, bake a batch of cookies and give them away, or donate your time or money to a worthy cause. Just do something and see how you feel afterwards.

2. Consider whether you are living a divided life or an undivided one. If you think you are living a divided life, what would it take for you to live an undivided one?

3. Think about what you can do for the environment. Choose one small thing, such as not eating meat or taking the bus to work, and make a commitment to do it for one week. It's a good idea to write it down and tell someone. After the week is over, reflect on whether or not you kept your word. If you did, give yourself a pat on the back and keep going. If you did not, don't feel guilty, but think about why you did not keep your commitment. Perhaps you chose something that was too difficult, perhaps you got distracted or apathetic, or perhaps you did not have enough time or energy. Whatever the reason, remind yourself about your commitment, modify it if you want to, and then try again.

CHAPTER 9

Persevering for the Long Haul

> *Great works are performed not by strength
> but by perseverance.*
>
> —— SAMUEL JOHNSON, *Rasselas*

PERSEVERANCE HELPS to nurture intrinsic hope because it gives us the determination to endure whatever happens. Perseverance persists—day after day, month after month, and year after year. Its stamina and fortitude are necessary to maintain and cultivate the habits of hope I've already discussed: being present, expressing gratitude, loving the world, accepting what is, and taking action. But more than this, perseverance is essential because it doesn't depend on achieving results. With perseverance, we can work to resolve the global eco-social crisis and build a better world without expecting to see the fruits of our efforts.

In these times, we need perseverance like never before. The crisis we face is more ominous than any other in human history. The stakes are higher and the likelihood of full-blown catastrophe greater. The task before us is massive. It's not only about working on individual problems, such as climate disruption or poverty, it's about working on their common causes. Responding to individual problems is important, but it's not enough because they are connected and share common roots. Not only are they all caused by the inherently harmful economic, political, and social systems that dominate Western culture, they are based on the misguided beliefs that underlie these systems. It is only by restructuring these systems and changing our cultural values that the crisis can be resolved. This may not be a task we can complete in our lifetimes, but with perseverance it is a task we can dedicate our lives to.

The task of remaking these systems and the beliefs that led to them requires enormous perseverance. Not only individual perseverance but collective perseverance. Although we all need personal stick-to-it-ness, the need for collective resolve is even more important. Our shared future is at stake, so we must work together across national, political, economic, social, and age differences. Responding to the global situation demands more than an individual sprint race or even a marathon. It requires an ongoing collaborative effort, in which everyone helps each other and the relay baton is passed from one generation to the next. This may sound like an impossible dream, but as things continue to fall apart humankind may well find the collective perseverance it needs.

We can nurture perseverance by reminding ourselves of others who have persevered. Indeed, human history is full of their stories. I think, for example, of Mohandas Gandhi, Rachel Carson, Wangari Maathai, and Nelson Mandela. They understood that social change rarely happens overnight and dedicated their lives to building a better world. I also think about whole populations who faced seemingly impossible odds and survived. The persistence of Moses and the Israelites who faced many disasters after they escaped from bondage in Egypt. The courage of countless African slaves who suffered unspeakable cruelty at the hands of their American and European oppressors. The endurance of tens of thousands of "Okies" who were forced to abandon their farms during the 1930s Dust Bowl and become migrant workers in California. And these examples are just the tip of the iceberg.

Throughout history, people have always worked together to ensure their common survival. Indeed, we are alive today only because previous generations persevered. Can we remember them and let their struggles give us strength? By understanding what they did, we can measure their efforts not only by whether they were successful, but also by their determination. In the same way, we can gauge our own efforts by the strength of our perseverance, regardless of whether we succeed or not.

I have witnessed many acts of collective perseverance. In 1985, when I was manager of the City of Toronto's Environmental Protection Office, I proposed that city council enact a right-to-know bylaw. This bylaw would have given residents the right to know what chemicals were being used, stored, and disposed of by businesses in their neighborhoods. It was strongly endorsed by environmental activists, local unions, and community groups. However, many businesses objected, as did the provincial government. Not surprisingly, the bylaw failed to pass. But those who supported it did not give up. They watched and waited for nearly 20 years, and when the political climate was more favorable they revived the idea. In 2003, the Toronto Environmental Alliance and the Toronto Cancer Prevention Coalition launched a major campaign in support of a right-to-know bylaw and after five years of lobbying they were successful. In 2008, more than 20 years after my original proposal, Toronto city council passed the Environmental Reporting and Disclosure Bylaw and became the first city in Canada to require businesses to report their use, manufacture, and discharges of toxic chemicals. This is amazing perseverance.

Whether it's collective or individual, there are at least three types of perseverance needed to respond to our situation and nurture intrinsic hope:

+ *endurance* to stay open to all the bad news about our environmental and social problems without being overwhelmed and falling into apathy or denial

+ *dedication* to continue to work with our fears and other difficult feelings about what's happening
+ *determination* to stay positive and taking action, despite setbacks and disappointments

These types of perseverance are interconnected. For instance, I worked on the health effects of toxic chemicals for much of the past 40 years and needed endurance to stay open to the emerging science. As more and more studies have documented the widespread effects of these substances, I needed dedication to continue to work with the fear, sadness, and grief I feel. And I needed determination to stay engaged and active, especially when I feel disappointed and frustrated.

Perseverance requires a purpose and a commitment (see Chapter Eight). Without them, there is no reason to stay the course. Unless we have a clear purpose and a strong commitment to work on it, we won't persevere. In other words, purpose and commitment arouse perseverance. But many today seem to lack these qualities. Some seem to lack any purpose or commitment at all, whether self-centered or altruistic. They live lives of quiet desperation, drifting aimlessly from one thing to another, feeling hopeless and alone. They have no reason to persevere. Others focus on their own happiness and rarely consider how to help other people or how their actions affect others. They may have a selfish type of perseverance but it lacks the altruistic motivation needed to persevere for the common good.

Self-Discipline

Another ingredient of perseverance is self-discipline. Self-discipline enables us to persevere through difficult times and cope with life's ups and downs. Unfortunately, it often gets a bad rap today. This is because of the way we think about it. For most people, self-discipline is about being hard on themselves and depriving themselves of pleasure and enjoyment. But it can be viewed more positively as the capacity to manage the conflicts in our minds, especially internal battles between our short-term desires and our long-term purposes. These types of conflicts are very common. We want to eat ice cream, but we also want to lose weight. We want to buy a new car, but we also want to save for retirement. We want to have fun with our friends, but we also want to help out at the homeless shelter. These conflicts are also very common when you think about environmental and social issues. We want a weed-free lawn, but we also want to protect the earth from toxic pesticides. We want to buy cheap clothes, but we also want the workers who make them to receive a fair wage. We want to jet off somewhere for an exotic vacation, but we also want to reduce our greenhouse gas emissions. In these and other similar conflicts, self-discipline can help us to stick with our purpose and commitment and not give into our short-term or selfish desires.

Self-discipline has another very important benefit: it makes people happy. We often think of self-disciplined people as being miserable, uptight, or bad-tempered, but the opposite is true. Self-disciplined people tend to be happier and more satisfied with their lives than those who are self-indulgent.[1] Are you surprised? It seems so counterintuitive. The reason is that self-discipline brings stability and structure into our lives, makes us more responsible, and helps us to overcome harmful habits and honor our purpose and commitment. Interestingly, self-disciplined people tend to avoid situations that lead to inner conflicts. They have the awareness to know what conditions and circumstances will trigger internal conflicts and steer clear of them. So although it's true that self-discipline requires effort, this is only a reflection of our tendency to focus on the difficulty of exercising it, rather than the benefits that result when we do.

Resilience

Resilience is necessary for perseverance because it helps us bounce back whenever we are knocked down by life. It's not that resilient people don't experience disappointments and setbacks. Rather, they have learned how to work with them. They know how to pick up the pieces and carry on. Like the proverbial phoenix that rises from the ashes, resilient people can remake themselves whenever life deals them a blow.

Resilience comes from accepting that life is constantly changing and that everything is impermanent. When we understand that nothing—absolutely nothing—is permanent, we can become more flexible and roll with the punches. It's easy to think that resilience comes from being tough and inflexible but the opposite is true. The more rigid we become, the less resilient we will be. That's why skyscrapers are designed to sway in the wind like trees. According to Kate Ascher, author of *The Heights: Anatomy of a Skyscraper*, "If a building weren't able to move at the top, then various structural elements might be damaged because of the wind pressure... In earthquake zones, (some buildings) will be designed to move a little bit on their foundations as well—so they don't take as much pressure as they would if they were absolutely static."[2] In other words, flexibility equals resilience.

Flexibility not only makes us more resilient, it also means that we can take advantage of new opportunities. Conversely, inflexibility means that we will probably miss them. The reason for this is simple—when we put our time and energy into maintaining the illusion of permanence, we cannot see the possibilities inherent in a situation. If we believe that everything stays the same, we won't be able to take advantage of the changes that are actually happening. In this way, holding onto the illusion of permanence makes it less likely that we will respond to our situation appropriately. To enhance our resilience and our perseverance, we need to accept the reality of change, notice whatever is happening, be flexible, and pay attention to emerging opportunities.

Long-Term Thinking

Long-term thinking helps to foster perseverance. This does not mean future-tripping or ignoring the present, but it does mean remembering those who will come after us. Many Native American tribes, such as the Iroquois, take a long-term view when they make decisions by taking into account how their actions will affect the seventh generation. Decisions that consider the consequences on future generations honor our responsibility to them and enable us to see our choices in the larger context of extended time.

For most of human history, people have considered the long-term future and been willing to work for things that would last. The ancient Egyptians built the pyramids to endure for millennia. In Europe, it took hundreds of years to build many of the medieval cathedrals and their builders never expected to see them completed. In the US, the Founding Fathers wrote the Constitution to guide the long-term development of a new society. Even in times of difficulty, humankind has always kept an eye on the long-term future.

But in the past century or so, Western culture seems to have lost this perspective. We tend to focus on tomorrow, next week, or next year. Rarely do we consider anything beyond a decade or two. The development of nuclear energy in the 1970s is a prime example. The fact that radioactive wastes will remain dangerous for hundreds of thousands of year was barely considered by those who approved this technology. Even today, there are no long-term management and disposal facilities in the US. When it comes to consumer products, many are designed to become obsolete after a few years. How old is your cell phone or TV? Most likely, less than five years old. In this throwaway society, we are taught to demand instant gratification. I remember a slogan used by Access, a UK credit card company that declared, "Take the waiting out of wanting." What does this say about long-term thinking? We want everything to be quick, easy, and convenient. Obsessed with the latest product, time-saving device or get-rich-quick scheme, we seem addicted to more-better-faster. We want everything and we want it NOW.

But short-term thinking erodes perseverance and intrinsic hope. In fact, it is a setup for hopelessness because when we encounter something that is difficult or requires significant time and effort, it is easy to think something like: "This isn't worth the bother." "This shouldn't be so hard." "I deserve to get what I want." "I should not have to wait for what I want." In contrast, long-term thinking says: "This is difficult, but it's worthwhile." In this way, long-term thinking helps us be content with taking one step at a time. This can be very freeing. Relieved of the burden of expecting to see the results of our efforts, we can wholeheartedly immerse ourselves in whatever needs to be done in the present moment.

Curiosity

Curiosity is essential for perseverance because it keeps us sitting on the edge of our seats wondering what will happen next. When we are curious we want to stick around to see how life unfolds. This makes perseverance much easier. Conversely, if we lose our curiosity and don't care about what happens next our perseverance will falter and fade, especially if our purpose and commitment aren't strong. Curiosity keeps us positive, open, and hopeful.

As a teacher, I always encourage my students to be curious. Although they often look to me for answers, I rarely give them because that's the easy way out. The world is full of answers. In fact, if you ask anyone a question you will probably get plenty of answers. Furthermore, everyone believes their answers are right. But how can we be certain about what is right? Because nothing is permanent, we can never reach a final conclusion about anything. All answers should be regarded as provisional and contingent on our ever-changing circumstances and conditions. Answers tend to shut down curiosity, while questions open it up. As Rainer Maria Rilke wrote in his *Letters to a Young Poet*, "I would like to beg you, dear Sir, as well as I can, to have patience with everything that is unresolved in your heart and to try to cherish the questions themselves, like closed rooms and like books written in a very strange tongue. Do not search now for the answers which cannot be given you because you could not live them. It is a matter of living everything. Live the questions now. Perhaps you will then gradually, without noticing it, one distant day live right into the answer."[3]

Sadly, Western culture often stifles curiosity because it teaches us to state our views and opinions, offer advice, and present information. As a society, we value debate and making statements over curiosity and inquiry. You don't have to believe me. In fact, I invite you to be curious about what I have just said. Do a little research for yourself by listening to two people talking about something—almost anything will do. After a few minutes, reflect on their conversation. Were they mostly stating their views and opinions, offering advice, or presenting information to each other? Or were they being curious and inquiring about what the other person thought or felt or the topic of the conversation? When I have done this, the results are nearly always the same. In most conversations, including my own, people tend to make statements to each other and are rarely truly curious. However, conversations based on stating opinions, offering advice, and presenting information can get boring and often lead to disagreements and misunderstandings. On the other hand, if we are curious and ask questions, we can learn more, deepen our relationships, create a shared understanding, and work together collaboratively. Again, you don't have to believe me. In fact, I encourage you to be curious about this statement and do some more research yourself.

Looking After Ourselves

If we want to persevere over the long haul, we need to look after ourselves. If we don't, we are likely to get exhausted and burn out. A well-known environmental activist once told me she felt an obligation to save the world. Like the Greek God Atlas, who carried the earth on his shoulders, she behaved as if she was supporting the entire weight of the planet on hers. She was a solo act—taking on every issue and working nearly 24/7. After a few years of frenetic activity, she had a breakdown. She did not look after herself and paid the price. These days, she takes time to look after herself and is a much more effective activist.

Many activists who work on ecological, social, and sustainability issues don't think about the sustainability of their own health and wellbeing. Often working long hours, they are stressed out, exhausted, or unwell. But then they can't look after the environment or other people. In fact, not only can they not help others, they become a liability because they need to be helped themselves. There is a good reason airplane flight attendants tell you to put on your own oxygen mask first before helping others.

Many activists think that all self-care is self-indulgent, but this isn't true because when we look after ourselves and stay healthy, we can work to benefit others. Self-care is only self-indulgent if we put ourselves at the center of concern and ignore the wellbeing of others. Parker Palmer put it this way: "Self-care is never a selfish act—it is simply good stewardship of the only gift I have, the gift I was put on earth to offer to others. Anytime we can listen to true self and give it the care it requires, we do so not only for ourselves but for the many others whose lives we touch."[4] Indeed, we can think of self-care as part of our responsibility to the planet. We are all made from the earth. Hence, looking after ourselves is one way in which we can look after her. When we look after ourselves and do it without harming the environment, we are fulfilling some of our responsibility to look after the planet.

Looking after ourselves is a form of self-discipline because it means recognizing our limits. Even though we might not want to acknowledge it, no one can do everything. None of us is superman or superwoman, even if we would like to be. We must listen to the inner wisdom of our bodies and keep ourselves healthy. This includes noticing when we need to rest. We all need time to rest, relax, and recuperate. Like letting a field lie fallow, human beings need down time too. This doesn't mean that nothing is happening. Far from it. Just as a fallow field is not inactive, neither is someone taking a break. In a fallow field, micro-organisms are busy breaking down dying and dead material, nutrients in the soil are being replenished, and wildlife populations are being restored. Similarly, for human beings lying fallow offers time to reflect and make sense of our lives, replenish our energy, and develop creative, new ideas. Looking after ourselves in this way is very healing and helps to build perseverance.

One of the best ways to look after ourselves is to have a personal practice—doing something on your own that nourishes your inner self. Meditating, praying, writing a journal, reading poetry, doing tai chi or yoga, are all examples. I have several regular personal practices that help me persevere. One is meditation. Nearly every morning, I meditate for at least 30 minutes. It's not a big deal. I just sit in a quiet place, become aware of my breath, and pay attention to the sensations, feelings, and thoughts in my body and mind (see the meditation instructions in Chapter Four). This simple practice enhances my awareness and relaxes me. It connects me with everyone and everything else that is breathing, as well as with all the plants and vegetation that are producing the oxygen I depend on. For me, meditation is one of the most profoundly self-nurturing experiences I know. Another of my practices is reconnecting with nature. This can be especially beneficial for people working on environmental issues. Every day, I try to take a walk outside or spend some time paying attention to the natural world. Even if it's only for a few minutes, this practice restores me. Like my meditation, it reminds me that I am part of the earth.

Celebrating Good News

Just as looking after ourselves can develop perseverance, so can celebrating good news. Celebrating helps us feel positive and strengthens our resolve to keep going. And like gratitude, it is the gift that keeps on giving because we can always look back on our celebration and feel good all over again. But as I discussed in Chapter Five, Western culture tends to ignore good news and focus on what's wrong. Indeed, it's almost automatic to dwell on what's wrong with the world rather than to celebrate what's good about it. And although it's true that humankind has a lot of problems, there is plenty of good environmental news to celebrate. For instance:

+ Emissions of greenhouse gases in the US have decreased by nine percent since 2005. Releases of carbon dioxide, methane, nitrous oxide, and other greenhouse gasses have all declined.[5]

+ In the 2015 Paris Agreement on climate change 195 countries signed up to limit their collective carbon emissions so that global warming will not exceed two degrees Celsius, with an aspiration to try and keep the increase to within 1.5 degrees above pre-industrial levels.

+ Investments in renewable energy sources hit a new record in 2015, totaling $286 billion, some three percent higher than the previous record in 2011. Moreover, in 2016 solar power became the cheapest form of electricity, about half the cost of coal.[6]

+ Sales of electric vehicles (EVs) are predicted to hit 41 million by 2040, representing 35 percent of new light-duty vehicle sales. During the 2020s EVs are expected to become more economical than gasoline or diesel cars in most countries.[7]

+ The ozone hole over the Antarctic is shrinking as a result of the Montreal Protocol on Substances that Deplete the Ozone Layer. According to Kofi Annan, former secretary general of the United Nations, the Montreal Protocol is "perhaps the single most successful international agreement to date."[8]

+ Blood lead levels in children have fallen dramatically since the imposition of controls on leaded gasoline in the US and other countries. Hailed as one of the most important public health achievements of the 20th century, this decrease has been linked with higher child IQs, increased productivity, and lower crime rates.

+ Acid rain levels have dropped significantly since the 1990s mostly because of regulations on emissions from coal, oil, and natural gas power plants. In Europe, sulfur dioxide emissions have been reduced by more than 70 percent, while in the US

they have been reduced by 40 percent. These reductions have
been achieved faster and at a lower cost than expected.[9]

+ Sustainable, responsible, and impact investing (SRI) continues
to grow very rapidly. In 2016, SRI investing in the US increased
to $8.72 trillion or about 20 percent of all investment funds
under professional management. This is an increase of 33 percent in just two years.[10]

That's a lot of good news! And there's plenty more, if we choose
to look for it.

In my professional life, I have had many reasons to celebrate
despite the disappointments I have encountered. I think of the
passage of the right-to-know bylaw I mentioned earlier in this
chapter, the work of the Environmental Protection Office that I
set up in Toronto in the 1980s, and all the wonderful students I
have had the privilege of teaching over the years. Their dedication
to building a better world is a source of much joy to me. You might
consider what you can celebrate. Whether it is a big thing or a
small one, celebrating good news is a great way to build perseverance and intrinsic hope.

I don't want to end this chapter without mentioning one more
ingredient in perseverance—being part of a strong, positive community. Not only can communities help us to love the world (see
Chapter Six), they can also enable us to persevere and stay engaged
in life. Just as it takes a village to raise a child, so it takes a community to persevere for the long haul. Whenever someone feels
hopeless, others can encourage them to keep on going. Whenever
someone feels depressed, their love and caring for others can give
them a reason to carry on. Whenever someone feels like giving up,
others can offer them inspiration and motivation. And by working together, we can all strengthen and sustain each other, thereby
nurturing perseverance and intrinsic hope.

Perseverance is its own reward. Even though there is no
guarantee that efforts to avert the global eco-social crisis will be

successful, doing what needs to be done can be immensely satisfying. Just being able to look back at the end of each day and say that we did our best and persevered can be enough to give us the determination to keep going. Perseverance is a journey without a beginning, a middle, or an end. It's what we are called to do in these times. It is what we need to nurture intrinsic hope. We may try and fail, but we cannot fail to try. There is no other positive response we can make.

✳ *Try This*

1. Whenever you feel like giving up, think about the perseverance of people like Mohandas Gandhi, Rachel Carson, Wangari Maathai, and Nelson Mandela. What would they do in your circumstances?

2. Start a daily personal practice to sustain your emotional, psychological, and spiritual health. Start small and grow it, as you are able.

3. Take a few minutes at the end of the day to identify at least one thing to celebrate. It could something you did, something that someone else did, or just something positive that happened.

Conclusion: Pandora's Gift

To CONCLUDE THIS BOOK, I'd like to consider the ancient Greek myth about Pandora and look at what it can tell us about hope. The story goes like this.

Once upon a time, Zeus, King of the Gods, asked his son Hephaestus, the god of craftsmen, to make a woman. Zeus called her Pandora and gave her to Epimetheus to be his wife. To celebrate their union, he gave the newlyweds a gift. Some say it was a box. Some say it was a jar. Whatever it was, Zeus forbade the young couple to open it.

One day, Epimetheus left Pandora for a few hours. While she was on her own she became curious about what was in the box. The more she thought about it, the more she longed to look inside. After all, what was the point of a gift you couldn't open? Maybe if she just took a quick peek. Looking around to make sure no one was watching Pandora opened the box just a crack. Immediately, all the pain and suffering known to humankind including fear, sorrow, despair, grief, anger, and hatred rushed out. She slammed the lid shut but it was too late. They had all escaped into the world.

Pandora burst into tears. As soon as Epimetheus heard her, he came running. As she told him what had happened, Pandora opened the lid completely to show him the box was empty. However, when she did this, they noticed there was something left at the bottom that had not escaped. It was hope.

Most interpretations of this well-known myth regard it as a story about the origins of pain and suffering and blame Pandora for what she did. But what if we reframe the story and see it from a different perspective? What if we see it as a story about intrinsic hope? Although Pandora released pain and suffering into the world, perhaps her swift action in slamming the lid shut prevented it from escaping. Could it be that Pandora actually preserved hope? Could it be that by preventing it from getting away she gave us a gift that can help us cope with our pain and suffering? Seen this way, Pandora is as much as heroine as a villain. Today, when the future looks very grim, she may have given us one of the greatest gifts ever given to humankind.

Just as hope stayed in Pandora's box, so it can live in our hearts. If we stay in the present moment, express gratitude for the gifts of life, love the world, accept whatever happens, take action, and persevere we will naturally feel more hopeful. Not hopeful that we will get what we want in the external world, but hopeful inside ourselves. Hopeful that we can work with life just as it is.

This intrinsic hope is increasingly important because we can no longer presume that humankind will be successful in resolving the global eco-social crisis. Given this, intrinsic hope offers the only constructive way forward. It says, "Yes, things look bad but we don't know for sure what will happen. We love life so let's do whatever we can." Intrinsic hope accepts the facts of the situation, but does not see them as the only truth or the whole truth. It recognizes that the future is uncertain, that anything could happen, and that our actions today could influence what actually happens. It understands that we may fail to stop the crisis, but we cannot sit idly by and do nothing.

I see this type of hope in the two Douglas fir trees outside my window. For decades, they have survived heat and cold, storms and droughts, and many different pests. Undaunted, these giants carry on making energy from the sun, drawing water from the ground, providing a home for other species, and offering shade to me and my neighbors. They do all this just because they are alive. Their intrinsic hope is constant and enduring. It just is. They remind me that I can be hopeful too, simply because I am alive, just like them.

That said, humankind needs a more capacious type of hope than Douglas fir trees because it must hold the knowledge that we are facing a catastrophe of our own making and that we can choose how to respond. And our choices matter. Really matter. We can choose to see the global eco-social crisis as a unique opportunity for transformation, as well as an unprecedented threat to human survival. We can choose to see the beauty and goodness in the world, as well as the pain and suffering. We can choose to see the proverbial glass as half full, as well as half empty. Intrinsic hope is about choosing to see all the possibilities. It's not about being optimistic or pessimistic and it's not about seeing the world as all bad or all good. It is about being willing to live in the uncertain terrain between these extremes—a middle way that doesn't depend on easy answers. This can feel strange and uncomfortable at first but it becomes easier with practice. All we need to do is be fully present, drop our storylines, and engage in the next moment with love and compassion.

Intrinsic hope is a choice we can each make every moment of our lives. We can't choose the circumstances of our birth and we may not have much choice about the circumstances of our death, but we can always choose our outlook on life. Victor Frankl, who survived the horrors of the Nazi concentration camps in the Second World War, said, "Everything can be taken from a man but one thing: the last of the human freedoms—to choose one's attitude in any given set of circumstances, to choose one's own way."[1] If he is right and the millions who suffered and died in concentration camps had the freedom to choose their attitude to life, then surely we have the freedom to choose ours today. But if we fail to make this choice and live in a world of extrinsic hope, fear and all the other painful feelings that come up when our hopes are disappointed will continue.

The awareness that we can choose our outlook on life is, I believe, related to human evolution, because at its root the crisis we face is about the evolution of human consciousness. As we collectively become more aware that our current ways of thinking and acting threaten our own survival and the survival of life on earth, we will realize that the future lies in our own hands—or rather, in our own minds. By rising above the illusion of separateness and aloneness, we will awaken to our interdependence on the web of life and uncover the human potential to act from love and compassion. Our task is to manifest this evolutionary change—for ourselves and for every other living being on the earth.

This sounds like a tall order, but we can make a start by uncovering and cultivating intrinsic hope. If we choose to act on what we love and refuse to be controlled by fear and other negative feelings, we will have an unshakeable faith in life and the will to act. Do you love hearing the songs of birds on a summer's morning? Then you can try to create the conditions in which birds will flourish. Do you love the taste of a fresh, locally grown tomato picked just in time for dinner? Then you can try to create the conditions in which you can do that. Do you love being in community with others? Then you can try to create the conditions in which communities will thrive. Letting your actions be motivated by the things you care about, rather than the things you fear is key to intrinsic hope.

Intrinsic hope is about letting our hearts be broken open by the pain and suffering of the world, so we can act from the love that lies underneath it all. Ask yourself, would you have feelings of sadness, despair, and grief if you did not love the world so passionately? Would you be afraid if you did not care for future generations so intensely? Would you grieve the loss of the natural landscapes of your childhood if they did not mean so much to you? I think not. Intrinsic hope is about digging deeper into the experience of being human, acknowledging the pain and suffering we inflict on each other and on the earth, and caring enough to take action. Not because we expect to succeed, but because it is the right thing, the only thing, to do in the circumstances. This is how to live courageously in these troubled times. And it is Pandora's gift to humankind.

Invitation

IF THE IDEAS IN THIS BOOK resonate with you, I invite you to send me your stories of intrinsic hope. They could be about your own experience of intrinsic hope as an individual or as part of a group or they could be about an example of intrinsic hope that you have witnessed. They could be about our environmental and social problems, but they don't have to be. I am interested in any stories about intrinsic hope, as I have described it in this book.

Please send your stories (no more than 500 words each, please) to me at: intrinsichope@gmail.com.

Thank you.

Acknowledgments

Writing and publishing a book is never a solo endeavor. This book is no exception. Without the assistance of many individuals and groups it would not have been possible.

First, I offer deep appreciation and respect to my Buddhist teachers, especially Dzigar Kongtrul Rinpoche, Pema Chodron, Joanna Macy, Jack Kornfield, Tara Brach, and His Holiness the Dalai Lama. Their generosity, kindness, and patience in offering the Buddha's teachings to me and others are truly amazing. I bow to you.

Many friends and colleagues contributed to the ideas in this book. Sometimes it was a casual conversation that led to a new insight, sometimes it was a comment or a remark that made me think differently, and sometimes it was the way they embody intrinsic hope in their lives. Whatever the particular contribution, I honor you all. In particular, I would like to thank Tom Ewell, Cathy Whitmire, Sarah Schmidt, Jeanne Strong, and other members of the Whidbey Island Friends Meeting (Quakers). The adult education sessions on hope that I led in 2015, 2016, and 2017 were very helpful as I was organizing and writing this book. I would also like to thank Jean MacGregor and the members of the Contemplative Practice and Sustainability Faculty Learning Community of the Curriculum for the Bioregion for encouraging me to try out some of my ideas in the classroom. Finally, I would like to acknowledge Larry Parks Daloz, Sharon Daloz Parks, and other members of the Whidbey Institute community. Your support over the years means more than I can say.

It has been my privilege to accompany and support many students of creative social change as they have struggled to remain hopeful. But although I was the supposed teacher and they were the students, I have learned an enormous amount from them. Witnessing their sorrows and joys, their achievements and setbacks, their smiles and tears, has taught me to be more hopeful. Furthermore, those who have taken classes with me since 2013 were sometimes unknowing participants in my inquiry on hope. You all made a very significant contribution to this book.

I want to honor those who reviewed an early version of this book, including Sally Elder, Karyn Lazarus, Rachel Lodge, and Janice O'Mahony. Your suggestions and comments helped me to express myself more clearly and to tighten up the manuscript considerably. Similarly, I would like to thank Rob West, Sue Custance, and the team at New Society Publishers for working with me to publish this book and bring the idea of intrinsic hope to a larger audience.

Finally, I offer my heart's gratitude to my husband George, my son Jonathan, and his wife Leslie. The ongoing blessings and gifts that I receive from each of you are an endless source of happiness and joy to me. Thank you.

Endnotes

Introduction

1. John Muir. *My First Summer in the Sierras* (Sierra Club Books 1988), p. 110.
2. Intergovernmental Panel on Climate Change. *Climate Change 2014: Impacts, Adaptation and Vulnerability. Summary for Policy Makers* (2014). ipcc.ch/report/ar5/wg2/
3. Ibid.
4. UN Factsheet on Water. un.org/waterforlifedecade/scarcity.shtml
5. Intelligence Community Assessment. *Global Water Security.* ICA 2012-08, February 2, 2012. dni.gov/files/documents/Newsroom /Press%20Releases/ICA_Global%20Water%20Security.pdf
6. World Wildlife Fund. *Living Planet Report 2016.* worldwildlife.org /pages/living-planet-report-2016
7. wwf.panda.org/about_our_earth/biodiversity/biodiversity
8. Daniel Hoornweg and Perinaz Bhada-Tataz. *What a Waste: A Global Review of Solid Waste Management.* Urban development series; knowledge papers no. 15. (2012) Washington, DC: World Bank. siteresources.worldbank.org/INTURBANDEVELOPMENT /Resources/336387-1334852610766/What_a_Waste2012_Final.pdf
9. rona.unep.org/regional-priorities/tackling-marine-debris
10. Jenna R. Jambeck, Roland Geyser, Chris Wilcox, et al., Plastic Waste Input from Land into the Ocean. *Science* 347 (6223):768–771 (Feb 13, 2015).
11. Krista Harper and S. Ravi Rajan. *International Environmental Justice: Building the Natural Assets of the World's Poor.* (Political Ecology Research Institute, 2004), University of Massachusetts at Amherst.
12. United Nations. *World Population Prospects: The 2017 Revision.* un.org/en/development/desa/publications/world-population -prospects-2015-revision.html
13. Falsely attributed to Chief Seattle by Ted Perry in a 1971 script for a program on ecology produced by the Southern Baptist Radio and Television Commission.

14. "The Mystique of the Earth," Thomas Berry, interviewed by Caroline Webb. *Caduceus* 59 (Spring 2003).

15. World Health Organization. *Preventing Disease Through Healthy Environments: Towards an Estimate of the Environmental Burden of Disease.* (2006).

16. Ian Gien. "Land and Sea Connection: The East Coast Fishery Closure, Unemployment and Health." *Canadian Journal of Public Health* 91(2) (2000): 121–124.

17. Erin Anderssen. "The Cod Collapse." *The UNESCO Courier: Research Library.* Vol. 51. (1998): p. 44–46.

18. John Aberth. *The Black Death: The Great Mortality of 1348–1350, A Brief History with Documents.* (Bedford/St. Martin's, 2005).

19. John Kelly. *The Great Mortality: An Intimate History of the Black Death, the Most Devastating Plague of All Time.* (Harper Perennial, 2005).

20. Jared Diamond. *Collapse: How Societies Choose to Fail or Succeed.* (Penguin Books, 2005).

21. *China Daily* February 21, 2014. china.org.cn/environment/2014-02/21/content_31545431.htm

22. Globescan. December 2016. *Globescan Radar Climate Change eBrief.*

23. Joe Tucci, Janise Mitchell, and Chris Goddard. *Children's Fears, Hopes and Heroes: Modern Childhood in Australia.* (Australian Childhood Foundation and the National Research Center for the Prevention of Child Abuse, 2007), Monash University.

24. Lise van Susteren and Kevin J. Coyle. *The Psychological Effects of Global Warming on the United States: And Why the U.S. Mental Health Care System Is Not Adequately Prepared.* (2012), National Wildlife Federation. nwf.org/~/media/PDFs/Global-Warming/Reports/Psych_Effects_Climate_Change_Full_3_23.ashx

25. Susan Clayton, Christie Manning, and Caroline Hodge. *Beyond Storms & Droughts: The Psychological Impacts of Climate Change.* (American Psychological Association and ecoAmerica, 2014).

26. Joanna Macy. "Working Through Environmental Despair." In *Ecopsychology: Restoring the Earth, Healing the Mind,* Theodore Roszak, Mary E. Gomes, and Allen D. Kanner (eds.) (Sierra Club Books, 1995), p. 241.

27. Thich Nhat Hanh. "The Bells of Mindfulness." In *Spiritual Ecology: The Cry of the Earth,* Llewellyn Vaughan-Lee (ed.) (The Golden Sufi Center, 2013), p. 25.

28. Therese Pettersson and Peter Wallensteen. "Armed Conflicts 1946–2014." *Journal of Peace Research* 52(4) (2016): 536–550.

29. Anxiety and Depression Association of America. adaa.org/under standing-anxiety

30. National Center for Health Statistics. "Antidepressant Use in People Aged Twelve and Over: United States 2011–2014." cdc.gov/nchs /data/databriefs/db283.htm

31. theguardian.com/society/2013/jun/19/anxiety-depression-office -national-statistics

32. Rubem Alves. *Tomorrow's Child: Imagination, Creativity, and the Rebirth of Culture.* (Harper & Row, 1972).

Chapter 1: Naming Our Feelings about the Global Eco-social Crisis

1. Starhawk. *Truth or Dare: Encounters with Power, Authority, and Mystery.* (Harper & Row, 1987), p.198.

2. World Commission on Environment and Development. *Our Common Future.* (Oxford University Press, 1987).

3. William Sloane Coffin. *Alive Now!* (May-June, 1993) p. 37.

4. Aldo Leopold. *A Sand County Almanac (Outdoor Essays and Reflections).* (Ballantine Books, 1987), p. 117.

5. Peter Howe, M. Mildenberger, J. Marlon, and A. Leiserowitz. *Yale Climate Opinion Maps—U.S. 2016,* Yale Program on Climate Change Communication. climatecommunication.yale.edu /visualizations-data/ycom-us-2016/

6. John Cook, et al. "Quantifying the Consensus on Anthropogenic Global Warming in the Scientific Literature." *Environmental Research Letters* 8 (2013).

7. George Marshall. *Don't Even Think About It: Why Our Brains Are Wired To Ignore Climate Change.* (Bloomsbury, 2014), p. 2.

8. *Yale Climate Opinion Maps.*

9. Robert Jay Lifton. "Beyond Psychic Numbing: A Call to Awareness." *American Journal of Orthopsychiatrics,* (1982): 52:4.

10. T. S. Eliot. "Burnt Norton." *The Four Quartets.* (Harcourt, 1968), p. 14.

Chapter 2: Reasons for Hope

1. Thomas R. Karl. *Key Challenges for Environmental Data and Information as Viewed from NCEI. Department of Commerce Data Advisory Council.* (2014) esa.doc.gov/cdac-presentation-key-challenges-for

-environmental-data-and-information-as-viewed-from-ncei-tom
-karl.pdf

2. US Fish and Wildlife Service. Bald Eagle. Fact Sheet: Natural History, Ecology, and History of Recovery, (2007, revised). fws.gov
    /midwest/eagle/uncovery/biologue.html

3. Colin Nickerson. "New England Sees Return of Forests, Wildlife."
    (Boston Globe, 2013). bostonglobe.com/metro/2013/08/31/new
    -england-sees-return-forests-and-wildlife/lJRxacvGcHeQDmtZ
    to9WvN/story.html

4. Thomas Berry. *The Great Work: Our Way into the Future*. (Random House, 2011), p. 82.

5. James Lovelock. *Gaia: A New Look at Life on Earth*. Oxford University Press, 1979).

6. Yue Wang. "More People Have Cell Phones than Toilets, UN Study Shows." (*Time Magazine*, 2013). newsfeed.time.com/2013/03/25
    /more-people-have-cell-phones-than-toilets-u-n-study-shows/

7. internetworldstats.com/stats.htm

8. International Environmental Agreements Database Project.
    iea.uoregon.edu/

9. Martin Luther King Jr. "Out of the Long Night." *The Gospel Messenge*, 1958. https://archive.org/details/gospelmessengerv107mors

10. Science and Environmental Health Network. Wingspread Conference on the Precautionary Principle, January 26, 1998. sehn.org
    /wing.html

11. Paul Hawken. *Blessed Unrest: How the Largest Social Movement in the World Came Into Being and Why No One Saw It Coming*. (Viking, 2007), p. 3.

12. Wendell Berry. "A Poem on Hope," in *Leavings*. (Counterpoint, 2010).

13. Oliver Goldsmith. *The Citizen of the World: or, Letters from a Chinese Philosopher, Residing in London, to His Friends in the East*. (Fredonia Books, 2004), Letter VII.

14. Adrienne Rich. "Natural Resources," in *Dream of a Common Language: Poems 1974–1977*. (W. W. Norton, 1978).

Chapter 3: Intrinsic and Extrinsic Hope

1. Vaclav Havel. *Disturbing the Peace*. (Vintage, 1990), p. 181.

2. Margaret Wheatley. "The Place Beyond Hope and Fear." *Shambhala Sun*. Spring, 2009.

3. Thich Nhat Hahn. *Peace in Every Step: The Path of Mindfulness in Every Step.* (Bantam Books, 1991), p. 41.
4. Psalms 46 verse 1–2. (Authorized Version.)
5. Romans 5:5. (A.V.)
6. Surah 65. At-Talaq, Ayah 3.
7. *The Bhagavad Gita.* (Translated for the Modern Reader by Eknath Easwaran.) (Nilgiri Press, 1985), Chapter 2 Verses 55–57.
8. Thomas Merton. *The Hidden Ground of Love: The Letters of Thomas Merton.* (Harcourt Brace Jovanovich, 1993), p. 292.
9. Thich Nhat Hanh. "The Miracle of Being Awake." *Yoga Journal*, July/August, 1984. p. 28.
10. David W. Orr. *Hope Is an Imperative: The Essential David Orr.* (Island Press, 2011), p. xix.
11. Frances Moore Lappé (in conversation with Fritjof Capra). 2013. "Hope is What We Become in Action." ecoliteracy.org/essays/hope -what-we-become-action-frances-moore-lappe-and-fritjof-capra -conversation
12. Thich Nhat Hanh. "The Miracle of Being Awake." *Yoga Journal*, July/August 1984, p. 28.

Chapter 4: Being Present

1. James Hillman. *The Thought of the Heart and the Soul of the World* (Spring Publications, 1992), p. 115.
2. Maggie Jackson. *Distracted: The Erosion of Attention and the Coming Dark Age* (Prometheus Books, 2008), p. 13–15.
3. Christopher Chabris and Daniel Simons. *The Invisible Gorilla: How Our Intuitions Deceive Us.* (Harmony, 2011).
4. Max Ehrmann. *The Desiderata of Happiness.* (Crown, 1995).
5. Rachel Carson. *The Sense of Wonder.* (Harper & Row, 1965), p. 42.
6. Carl Sagan. *Cosmos: A Personal Journey.* TV series aired in 1980. Quote is taken from the first episode, "The Shores of the Cosmic Ocean."
7. Thomas Berry. *The Dream of the Earth.* (Sierra Club Books, 1988), p. 132.

Chapter 5: Expressing Gratitude

1. Michael E. McCollough, Robert Emmons, and Jo-Ann Tsang. "The Grateful Disposition: A Conceptual and Empirical Topography." *Journal of Personality and Social Psychology* (2002): 82(1): 112–127.

2. Margarita Engle. *The Firefly Letters: A Suffragette's Journey to Cuba.* (Henry Holt and Co., 2010), p. 141.

3. Robert Emmons. *Thanks! How the New Science of Gratitude Can Make You Happier.* (Houghton Mifflin Harcourt, 2007).

4. Robert A. Emmons and Michael E. McCollough. "Counting Blessings Versus Burdens: An Experimental Investigation of Gratitude and Subjective Well-Being in Daily Life." *Journal of Personality and Social Psychology,* (2002): 84(2): 377–389.

5. John W. Gardner. Speech given in 1965, as quoted in John Gardner, *Uncommon American.* pbs.org/johngardner/sections/writings

6. Christopher Fry. *A Sleep of Prisoners.* (Dramatists Play Service, 1998).

7. John Kretzmann and John McKnight. *Building Communities from the Inside Out: A Path Towards Finding and Mobilizing a Community's Assets.* (ACTA Publications, 1993).

8. G.K. Chesterton. *St. Francis of Assisi.* (Doran, 1924), p. 114.

9. Pema Chodron. *The Wisdom of No Escape.* (Shambhala Press, 2001), p. 25.

10. Worldwide Fund for Nature. *Living Planet Report 2016.* Gland, Switzerland (2016).

11. Victor Lebow. "Price Competition in 1955." *Journal of Retailing.* 31(1) Spring 1955.

12. Tim Kasser. *The High Price of Materialism.* (MIT Press, 2002).

13. New Economics Foundation. *The Happy Planet Index: 2016 Report.* happyplanetindex.org/

Chapter 6: Loving the World

1. Erich Fromm. *The Anatomy of Human Destructiveness,* New York (Holt, Rinehart and Winston) 1973, p. 366.

2. Edward O. Wilson. *Biophilia.* (Harvard University Press, 1986), p. 1.

3. Ibid, p. 1.

4. Howard Eves. *Mathematical Circles Adieu.* (Prindle, Weber & Schmidt, 1977).

5. Humane Society of the United States. *Farm Animal Statistics: Slaughter Totals.* humanesociety.org/news/resources/research/stats_slaughter_totals.html

6. Robert Goodland and Jeff Anhang. "Livestock and Climate Change: What If the Key Actors in Climate Change are Cows, Pigs, and

Chickens?" *World Watch Magazine* November/December 2009, p. 10–19.

7. Food and Agriculture Organization. 22 March 2007. "FAO urges action to cope with increasing water scarcity." fao.org/newsroom/en /news/2007/1000520/index.Html

8. David Pimental et al., "Water Resources: Agriculture, the Environment, and Society." *Bioscience* 47 (2), 97–106 (1997).

9. Jonathan Safran Foer. *Eating Animals.* (Little, Brown, 2009).

10. Robert Putnam. *Bowling Alone: The Collapse and Revival of American Community.* (Simon & Schuster, 2000).

11. Robert L. Thayer. *Lifeplace: Bioregional Thought and Practice.* (University of California Press, 2003), p. 5.

12. This quiz is based on an earlier one called "Where Are You At?" developed by Leonard Charles, Jim Dodge, Lynn Milliman, and Victoria Stockley, in *Coevolution Quarterly* Vol. 32 (Winter 1981), p. 1.

13. P. Emrath, "How Long Buyers Remain in Their Homes." National Association of Home Builders. February 11, 2009.

14. Vicki Robin. *Blessing the Hands That Feed Us: What Eating Closer to Home Can Teach Us About Food, Community, and Our Place on Earth.* (Viking Press, 2014), p. 253.

15. Edgar Mitchell. *The Way of the Explorer: An Apollo Astronaut's Journey through the Material and Mystical Worlds.* (New Page Books, 2008, rev. ed.), p. 288.

16. Kevin W. Kelley (ed.). *The Home Planet.* (Addison-Wesley, 1988).

17. Thomas Berry and Mary Evelyn Tucker. *Evening Thoughts.* (Counterpoint Press, 2010), p. 43.

18. As quoted on "Ely Parker 1844–1865. Seven Generations—The Role of Chief." pbs.org/warrior/content/timeline/opendoor/roleOfChief .html

19. Jo Cofino. "How Women Became Stars in the Battle Against Climate Change". *Huffington Post.* January 27, 2016. huffingtonpost .com/entry/how-love-really-did-change-the-course-of-history _us_56a8b7a7e4b0f71799928722d

Chapter 7: Accepting What Is

1. J. Cook, et al., "Consensus on Consensus: A Synthesis of Consensus Estimates on Human-Caused Global Warming." *Environmental Research Letters* 11:4 (13 April 2016).

2. 11:15 am, November 6, 2012. https://twitter.com/realdonaldtrump/status/265895292191248385?lang=en

3. Joanna Macy. "Taking Heart: Spiritual Exercises for Social Activists," in Fred Eppsteiner (ed.), *The Path of Compassion: Writings on Socially Engaged Buddhism*, (Parallax Press, 1988), p. 207.

4. Joanna Macy and Chris Johnstone. *Active Hope*. (New World Library, 2012), p. 69–70.

5. Kahlil Gibran. *The Prophet*. (Heinemann, 1973).

6. workthatreconnects.org

7. Attributed to Reinhold Niebuhr and used by Alcoholics Anonymous and other twelve step programs.

Chapter 8: Taking Action

1. Kate Davies. "Human Exposure Routes to Selected Persistent Toxic Chemicals in the Great Lakes Basin: A Case Study." (1988). *Proceedings of the Second World Conference on Large Lakes*. (Held on at Mackinac Island, Michigan, May 1986.)

2. Kate Davies. "Concentrations and Dietary Intake of Organochlorines Including PCBs, PCDDs and PCDFs in Fresh Food Composites Grown in Ontario, Canada." *Chemosphere* 17 (2), (1988): 263–276.

3. Kate Davies. "Human Exposure Pathways to Selected Organochlorines and PCBs in Toronto and Southern Ontario." *Advances in Environmental Science and Technology* (1990) 23: 275–282 (ed. J. Nriargu).

4. Parker Palmer. *A Hidden Wholeness: The Journey Towards an Undivided Life*, (Jossey-Bass, 1999).

5. Parker Palmer. *Let Your Life Speak: Listening for the Voice of Vocation*, (Jossey-Bass, 2000), p. 2–3.

6. Laurent A. Parks Daloz, Cheryl H. Keen, James P. Keen, and Sharon Daloz Parks. *Common Fire: Leading Lives of Commitment in a Complex World*, (Beacon Press, 1996), p. 195–196.

7. Derrick Jensen. "Forget Shorter Showers." *Orion Magazine*, (July 8 2009). orionmagazine.org/article/forget-shorter-showers

8. Malcolm Gladwell. *The Tipping Point*, (Back Bay Books, 2002).

9. William James. *The Letters of William James, Volume 2*, ed. Henry James, (Kessinger Publishing, 1926), p. 90.

Chapter 9: Persevering for the Long Haul

1. W. Hofman et al. "Yes, But Are They Happy? Effects of Trait Self-Control on Affective Wellbeing and Life Satisfaction." *Journal of Personality* 82(4): 265–277 (2014).

2. "How the World's Tallest Skyscrapers Work." Interview with Kate Ascher by Terry Gross, November 7, 2011. npr.org/2011/11/07/141858484/how-the-worlds-tallest-skyscrapers-work

3. Rainer Maria Rilke. *Letters to a Young Poet.* Letter IV. (BN Publishing, 2008), p. 21.

4. Parker Palmer. *Let Your Life Speak: Listening for the Voice of Vocation.* (Jossey-Bass, 2000), p. 30.

5. US EPA. *Climate Change Indicators in the United States: U.S. Greenhouse Gas Emissions* (updated May 2014). epa.gov/climate-indicators/climate-change-indicators-us-greenhouse-gas-emissions

6. World Economic Forum. *Renewable Infrastructure Investment Handbook: A Guide for Institutional Investors.* December 2016. www3.weforum.org/docs/WEF_Renewable_Infrastructure_Investment_Handbook.pdf

7. Bloomberg New Energy Finance, February 25, 2016. https://about.bnef.com/blog/electric-vehicles-to-be-35-of-global-new-car-sales-by-2040

8. *International Day for the Preservation of the Ozone Layer—16 September.* United Nations. un.org/en/events/ozoneday/background.shtml

9. Comparison of the E.U. and U.S. Approaches Towards Acidification, Eutrophication and Ground Level Ozone. Case Study 1. Assessment of the Effectiveness of European Air Quality Policies and Measures (October 4, 2004) ec.europa.eu/environment/archives/cafe/activities/pdf/case_study1.pdf

10. US SIF. *Report on U.S. Sustainable, Responsible and Impact Investing Trends 2016.* Washington, D.C.

Conclusion: Pandora's Gift

1. Victor Frankl. *Man's Search for Meaning: An Introduction to Logotherapy.* (Simon & Schuster Touchstone Edition 1984), p. 75.

About the Author

KATE DAVIES, MA, DPhil, has worked on environmental and social issues for her entire career. She set up and managed the City of Toronto's Environmental Protection Office and established and directed a successful environmental policy consulting company. She is currently clinical associate professor in the School of Public Health at the University of Washington,  emeritus faculty at Antioch University, and senior fellow at the Whidbey Institute. Her written work has been published in newspapers, magazines, and, journals across North America and internationally. Her first book, *The Rise of the U.S. Environmental Health Movement*, was selected by Booklist as one of the top ten books on sustainability published in 2013. Kate lives in Langley, WA.

ABOUT NEW SOCIETY PUBLISHERS

New Society Publishers is an activist, solutions-oriented publisher focused on publishing books for a world of change. Our books offer tips, tools, and insights from leading experts in sustainable building, homesteading, climate change, environment, conscientious commerce, renewable energy, and more—positive solutions for troubled times.

We're proud to hold to the highest environmental and social standards of any publisher in North America. This is why some of our books might cost a little more. We think it's worth it!

- We print all our books in North America, never overseas

- All our books are printed on **100% post-consumer recycled paper**, processed chlorine-free, with low-VOC vegetable-based inks (since 2002)

- Our corporate structure is an innovative employee shareholder agreement, so we're one-third employee-owned (since 2015)

- We're carbon-neutral (since 2006)

- We're certified as a B Corporation (since 2016)

At New Society Publishers, we care deeply about *what* we publish—but also about *how* we do business.

Download our catalogue at https://newsociety.com/Our-Catalog or for a printed copy please email info@newsocietypub.com or call 1-800-567-6772 ext 111

New Society Publishers
ENVIRONMENTAL BENEFITS STATEMENT

For every 5,000 books printed, New Society saves the following resources:[1]

20	Trees
1,841	Pounds of Solid Waste
2,026	Gallons of Water
2,643	Kilowatt Hours of Electricity
3,347	Pounds of Greenhouse Gases
14	Pounds of HAPs, VOCs, and AOX Combined
5	Cubic Yards of Landfill Space

[1] Environmental benefits are calculated based on research done by the Environmental Defense Fund and other members of the Paper Task Force who study the environmental impacts of the paper industry.

MIX
Paper from responsible sources
FSC® C016245
www.fsc.org

new society
PUBLISHERS
www.newsociety.com